Fifty Years in 13 Days

Fifty Years in 13 Days

Copyright 2009 Katie DeCosse & Jackie Maher

WOW! Publishing Group, Inc.
2359 Cleveland Street NE,
Minneapolis, MN 55418

First Edition

ISBN: 1-4382-5453-9

EAN-13: 97-81438-25453-1

All rights reserved. No part of this book may be reproduced, stored in a retrieval system, or transmitted in any form or by any means – electronic, mechanical, digital, photocopy, recording, or any other – except for brief quotations in printed reviews, without the prior permission of the author(s).

Printed in the United States of America

Reader comments

"As a mother, I could identify with Jackie and felt my heart rip in two when I read Jackie's story of birth and surrender."

LaRae Thompson

"I am 61 so know many women who were in Jackie's position in the sixties and have watched their lives and life stories unfold, with that unknown child often at the very center."

Margaret Nelson Brinkhaus

"The two of you have built such an amazing relationship in such a short period of time; I think it will give hope to those that are considering contact."

Kristie Maloney

"As I grow older, coming up on seventy-two, I realize more and more how really short life is and that you two finally came together is a blessing."

Barbara Marystone

"The writing was easy to read and very clear and the story itself is simply amazing, very uplifting."

Kim DeRoche

"It could have been so much worse"

Tim Maher

Fifty Years In 13 Days

A Mother/Daughter Reunion

Katie DeCosse

&

Jackie Maher

*Lois —
Enjoy the read and have a great summer.
Jackie Maher
Katie DeCosse*

Authors' note:

We have used several different fonts in the book to indicate who is "speaking" at the time.

Jackie will look like this

and Katie like this.

Combined narration will look like this. We hope this makes it easier for you to sink in and simply enjoy the read!

Preface

"I am a birth mother."

There. I have said it and it feels good. After fifty years of silence the secret is out. The shame is that I needed to keep it hidden for all of those years.

I was a victim of the 1950's mentality toward unwed motherhood. We had committed the sin that was nearly unforgivable. The world said we were bad and we bought it. We deserved to be shunned - to be put out of our homes and schools and we had no one to blame but ourselves. That is what they said. And who were they? They were our parents, teachers, friends, clergy, and anyone else who felt it gave them a leg up in the pecking order. We only did what a lot of young people did not get "caught" doing.

Luckily the father of my child had the foresight to see the handwriting on the wall. He saw the bleakness of a future together whereas I was blinded by my desire to raise my child in a safe, secure, two-parent home. I was wrapped up in a dream of "happily ever after" and refused to see that this was not a viable option. The only wise solution was to place my child for adoption so as to save her the awful stigma of illegitimacy and a life of poverty and uncertainty for I had no illusions about my capabilities as a single parent of the 50's.

I entered the Catholic Infants Home just weeks before my baby, a daughter arrived. A small number of women were able to make arrangements to keep their babies. That solution was not available to me. Most of us were sent home with empty arms. We were encouraged to forget about this experience and get on with our lives.

Did we really believe this was possible? We earnestly tried to forget. We came out of the home for unwed mothers and started to reclaim our identities. We pocketed our grief, took back our names, found new jobs, and made new friends. We tried to gain back our respect for ourselves and the respect of others. We worked hard.

In the vernacular of today, I redefined myself. Only twice in the ensuing years did I speak of this time in my life and then only briefly. I jealously guarded my secret. I wrapped my grief and anger around it to protect it from those who would shun my secret, my baby, and me.

Years became decades and somewhere along the way the rules changed. Adoption became "open" and single parenthood was no longer an aberration. Unwed mother became an antiquated term. And somewhere there was a woman, someone's daughter, my daughter, perhaps an adoptee in search of her birth parent. Meanwhile, as I raised my other five children, this daughter resided in the shadows of my memory and, as the song goes, "ever gentle on my mind."

Then one day my seventieth birthday passed and the loose ends of my life began clamoring for attention, for resolution. I needed to put my identifiable information on record in case my daughter needed it. I also had to inform my children of my long kept secret. Finally we could talk openly about the situation. And from some of my children came, "WOW! Mom, that is so exciting". Some were more cautious. But "exciting"? Where had I been? When had this happened? What about the shame?

My concern was that I might not have many years left, and what if I had answers that my daughter had been looking for? How was her health? Was she looking for genealogical roots? And might she be angry with me for waiting so long? And the worst case scenario, had she already passed away? It was time for me to know, to give and receive answers to the questions that lay between us.

Getting to know each other has been like a rebirth. My daughter and I have so many years to recover - fifty to be exact. I could not have imagined the response that my letter would bring. And the rewards have been phenomenal. The pain and sacrifices of fifty years ago have paled in the light of the joy we have discovered in getting to know each other.

I wish all stories could unfold like ours. But, that is not meant to be. Some parents prefer to stay hidden. Some adoptees do not wish to be found. And in spite of everything, even our road has its bumps. A lot of lives have been affected. Family dynamics have changed in spite of the fact that we have tried to make this transition as smooth as possible.

People have said that I am brave to have come out at this late date with our story. I am not sure if my move required bravery. It may have been a courageous act. I only know that for us, it was the right thing at the right time. Now I wonder why the fear and hesitation: this experience has brought so much happiness and closure. I have discovered that signing the papers does not sever *the bond between mother and child. In 1957 I did what I needed to do for my child. This new experience, this reunion feels like the circle is complete.*

I am glad that my generation is now able to come out of the closet. That those of us who want to, who need to, can make contact with the children we surrendered; that we can get answers to the nagging questions of where they are, and how they are, and are they happy. This is the final closure.

Folly Girls 2007

Our magical journey of reunion began long before I was even aware that my life was about to change so dramatically. For several years I had been looking forward to turning 50. I saw it as an age of empowerment, of maturity and freedom. In those final months leading up to 50, I became more comfortable in my own skin, saw joy more often than sadness, found ways to brighten up my life and found my authentic laugh. I was ready for whatever 50 had in store for me.

The celebration was planned and included a party, a trip to Folly Beach, SC and as the grand finale, a tattoo to honor the milestone of reaching 50. After that, my life would settle into a new normal.

The week in Folly Beach was an experience like no other. I invited 8 women to join me in an ocean front house for a week of celebration. The intent of this week was to celebrate turning 50 of course, but it was also an opportunity to spend time with girlfriends! The days were filled with laughter, good food, lots of "girl talk", walks on the beach, and "porch time", our favorite gathering place.

It would be impossible for that many women to gather and not talk about their mothers. We were no different. Some of our mothers are gone already, others elderly with varying degrees of ailments as would be expected. I am certain that part of each day was spent in sharing our mother experiences.

Having the ocean at our doorstep was soothing and life affirming. We all came away from that week renewed, rejuvenated, and changed in some way. In that week I came to accept and love myself for who I am. My new mantra became, "I am good enough for me, and that is good enough!"

On May 14, 2007 I received a document in the mail that changed my life forever. It was a letter from my birth mother. At the age of 50 I was given the opportunity to reconnect with the woman who gave birth to me.

Very few adoptees will receive such a letter at this age; most reunions take place earlier in life and with the prevalence of open adoptions, the need to reunite will eventually become a thing of the past. Unbeknownst to any of us at the time, the "Folly Girls" gave me the strength and confidence to go into this reunion experience with an open heart and mind; willing to take the risk, knowing that whatever the outcome of this journey, I would be OK!

Folly Girls 2007: Patty, Sharon, Teresa, Shirley, Paula, Katie, Tracey and Sally. Not Pictured: Kristie

The Letter

May 12, 2007*

Dear Katie,

    I am sure this letter is coming as a surprise to you. I recently initiated a private search to locate a daughter I surrendered for adoption in 1957. The search culminated in finding you. You were born on April 3, 1957 in St. Joseph Hospital in St. Paul, Minnesota. I surrendered my parental rights in early May of that year. I was recently able to obtain my papers from the agency so much of the information is renewed for me and some I never knew.

    If you are wondering why I chose to search at this late date, let me just say that suddenly all of the obstacles fell away and I found good people to advise me and help me in my search. My gratitude to them is eternal.

    To better introduce myself let me give you some information on my life today. My husband and I raised 5 children and a number of dogs and cats. We are both 71 years old and retired for the most part. By that I mean we are active, each with our own interests. He still maintains an interest in his chosen field of veterinary medicine. My interests include golf, which I just took up a few years ago. I am not good but do enjoy 9 holes now and again. I also love to read and have since first grade. I cannot pass a bookstore and have many books in my collection waiting to be finished. I also began creative writing just a few years ago and am told that my stuff is pretty good though I am not convinced. I belong to 3 card clubs, 500 and canasta, and enjoy outings with friends. My husband and I have done some extensive traveling over the years and I have recently discovered that I like traveling alone also. My philosophy is "He travels fastest who travels alone." Not my saying but it fits me well I think. I am also interested in philosophy by the way; my own and that of some of the major thinkers.

What else can I say? I would like to know more about your life if you see fit to have contact. I am concerned that I can perhaps answer any health issues you may have or questions about ancestry. There is a lot of Irish here. Any other questions you might have I would be glad to fill in the blanks. Perhaps we could meet over a cup of coffee or. . . . It has been my prayer all of these years that you have had a good and loving home. It is the wish of all birth mothers I believe when we find that we cannot keep our child. Would you let me know soon whether you wish contact or not? I thank you for that.

I am looking forward to hearing from you. Take care.

Love,
Jackie

PS – I timed this letter so as not to impose on any Mother's Day traditions you might be observing.

*Jackie signed the final adoption papers on May 12, 1957!

Response

May 14, 2007   9 PM

Dear Jackie,

    Wow. And I thought it was all downhill now that my 50th birthday celebration is officially over. As is typical for me I am in a fugue state between information and comprehension; it generally takes 12-18 hours for BIG news to sink in. However, I know you have been thinking of this for a lot longer than I have so I won't keep you hanging. In fact, if you are like me, you want an answer now.

    I have never seriously considered searching for you but have always been open to the prospect of a meeting should you initiate it. To what degree I can't say at this time however, I will take this opportunity to tell you a little bit about myself.

    I am currently the Clinical Training Coordinator and an instructor in the Veterinary Technology program at a local university. Briefly, my background in vet med is a degree from MIM followed by 16 years as a veterinary technician in small animal clinics. I began my teaching career in September of 2001, the 11th to be exact.

I live with my husband, dog and cat and have 2 grown stepchildren with children of their own. My stepdaughter was adopted by my husband and his first wife so we share that special connection. My husband, being 18 years older than I am, is retired from his career as a Social Worker. For various reasons I chose to not have children of my own so alas, no long lost grandchildren.

My life story will have to keep for another day but suffice it to say that I had every advantage available in the way of education and opportunity. I have one older brother and one younger sister who were also adopted. Both of my parents are very creative, artistic people and that has lent itself to a very interesting life.

We seem to share some common interests. I too, cannot pass a bookstore without going in. Mysteries are my favorite these days so it didn't take long to recall a phone call my husband received the other day from a Tim Maher - a half brother perhaps? I have stacks of books waiting to be read. I also enjoy crafts; crocheting and silk flower arranging are my current interests. I too enjoy writing and have been told that I am quite good at it.

I have been fortunate in my good health in spite of a nasty addiction to cigarettes. I have had a varied career starting out with a degree in Social Work. I am currently attending St. Mary's and working toward a Master's degree in Education. I like to travel and my most recent vacation was a week in an ocean front house with 8 other women in Folly Beach, SC. This was to celebrate 50th birthdays for 3 of us.

Anyway, that's me in a nutshell. I look forward to corresponding by email for now and am sure that at some point we will meet face to face. I have attached a picture for you. It is almost 2 years old but still a good likeness. The dog on the left is my beloved Winston.

I look forward to our journey,
Katie

Puccini, Katie and Winston

May 15-19, 2007

Hi, Katie,

Thank you for your quick response to my letter. I am glad that you were receptive and know that this was a bolt out of the blue for you. Also, I want to belatedly wish you a Happy Birthday.

I thought of you many times on that day. And I don't need to tell you how happy I am that you have had a good home and presumably a good life. When I started this process I only meant to put my information out there in case you ever looked for it. Then wait and see. Somewhere along the way this thing took on a life of its own and became a full blown search. People kept finding me who wanted to help and knew the ropes. One time I thought I had to let it go for awhile but another door opened and I dashed right through it. I guess it was just meant to be and this was the time to do it.

I loved your picture by the way. Blue eyes huh? Out of three tries I have not been able to produce a brown-eyed daughter to save my soul. I can't say the same for the boys.

It is quite a coincidence that you are a veterinary technician. My husband established Brooklyn Park Pet Hospital (BPPH) in the '70s. Then a few years later he opened Camden Pet Hospital. He sold BPPH in about 1990 and Camden in 1994 when he became ill and no longer felt competent to handle animals. He also spent 25 years supervising animal care at the Humane Society. Never ran into the "bugger" heh? Your pups are sooo cute!

I am currently taking writing classes at North Hennepin Community College from Louise Wyly. A few years ago, in one of her Memoir writing classes, I met a lady who suggested we start a writers group. So we did, just the two of us. We soon found a third and only this month added a fourth and think our group is complete. It is more like group therapy as once one starts digging into the past all sorts of memories surface and some of them not too friendly. But it is a fun group and we have been most supportive of each other.

I only within the last month opened up about my being a birth mother. The last member we incorporated is an adoptee and instrumental in my search. See how things happen? It is amazing! I also put together a book of memories for my family. Being the oldest of five, I remember things they never knew. It is only the first 20 years but I thought my kids might also have some questions one day when I am no longer here to answer them.

I don't want to go on too long but, about books. I also like a good mystery and have read all of Grafton and Evanovich. I also like William Kent Krueger, a Minnesota writer whom you might investigate if you haven't already. I recently finished SCENT OF GOD which is autobiographical and very good with a surprise ending. It is by Beryl Bissell who also has migrated to Minnesota. So who do you favor these days? This letter could go on and on and probably will if I don't do something about it. I hope to hear from you again, at your convenience, as there is much more I want to share. Take care, Katie.

Love, Jackie

Dear Jackie,

The shock of receiving your letter is wearing off and the information is starting to sink in. While I am looking forward to continued contact I have one enormous task to complete. I must tell Mom that the letter that she hoped would never come and perhaps assumed that at this late date never would, has arrived. This will be very difficult for her because quite frankly, I am the light of her life - those are her words.

I know exactly how she will feel but also know that eventually she will be fine. When my stepdaughter, Lynn, searched for her birth parents, it was very scary for her dad and me. Our fear was that we wouldn't measure up, that she would leave us. None of that came to pass and eventually life returned to "normal". Mom will get to that point too. I plan on talking to her this weekend and will let you know how it goes.

I suspect that you are practically bursting at the seams to tell me lots of things. Well, let 'er rip as they say. If you are able to at this time, it might be helpful to me if you could tell me a little bit about your life when you found out you were pregnant with me, your decision process and what it was like to "give me up". I would also be interested to hear what the intervening years were like; your hopes, fears, thoughts, etc. Also, do your children know about me? Have they always known? What do they think? Have you carried this "secret" privately all these years? What would you have named me? (This last question has been the most frequently asked question of the past two days as I share this news with those who are dear to me.) Please tell me as much of your story as you are comfortable with at this time.

I have shared your letter and email with my husband and several very dear friends. They have each commented on how your writing style and sense of humor sounds a lot like me! I look forward to reading more messages and think that it will ease us into our first meeting whenever that occurs. I am looking forward to that day with interest, fear and a sense of adventure for it will be a new adventure for both of us. Several years ago my dad gave me a photo album of pictures from when I was a baby and young child; many of the pictures were new to me and I think you will love to see them. My father spent many years in the advertising business - you may remember the Hamm's Bear - he was one of 3 people who drew all the ads for Hamm's. Anyway, his main artistic talent lies in the area of photography and so, like the barefoot children of cobblers, there are very few pictures of me as a child but the ones that I have are fabulous.

Okay, back to me! I have read all the Grafton's and Evanovich's as well - the grandma is one of my favorite characters of all! I have also read Krueger although I have not kept up with that series. Some of my other favorite mystery authors include Elizabeth George, Linda Barnes, Michael Connelly, John Sandford (local author), Robert Crais, Dennis Lehane, Anne Perry, Jan Burke, KJ Ericson (also local) and Virginia Lanier who wrote a series on bloodhound search and rescue which I highly recommend. Her first one, *Death in Bloodhound Red*, is a true page-turner! At this time I seem to be reading a lot of southern fiction. Right now I am in the midst of "Wish You Well", a beautifully written book by David Baldacci who usually writes legal thrillers. This is quite a departure for him and well worth the time.

I talked at length the other night with Lynn and she recommended the book called "The Girls Who Went Away" (2006) by Anne Fessler; perhaps you have read it? I have ordered it from Amazon with overnight delivery. It is a book about unwed mothers before Roe v. Wade. I am looking forward to reading the stories of these women, just like you, who found themselves with few choices for their unborn children and what that was like. I have always known I was adopted and in fact, worked part-time at Seton Center after I graduated from the College of St. Catherine with a degree in Social Work. I helped with the childbirth education classes and was a group leader for the single moms. It was very interesting work for me as an adoptee. Adoption has always been a topic near and dear to my heart and I am very comfortable talking about it.

I seem to be rambling on here and will close shortly. I just want you to know that I can appreciate, at least to some degree, the difficulty of your situation 50 years ago and thank you for making the decision to place me for adoption even though I suspect you found yourself with very few options. You obviously took good care of yourself while you were pregnant and gave birth to a healthy baby with all 10 fingers and toes and I thank you for that too. Did you get a chance to hold me? I'm a lot bigger now!

Take care and write whenever you like. I will try to respond accordingly but if you don't hear from me for a couple days, please don't worry; I won't change my mind about continued contact. Part of this journey is mine alone and there may be times when I need to do some sorting out of things on my own. I found it interesting that the quote about traveling alone fits you. I too, am a bit of a loner; I cherish my times of solitude.

Katie

PS - Thank you for the comments about the dogs. Actually, Winston is the one on the right - the Cavalier King Charles Spaniel. Puccini (the poodle) was a visitor that week and so was included in the photo. I always had trouble as a child remembering left from right and apparently still have lapses. The sunflowers in the background represent me as well for they are my favorite flower. I even had one tattooed on my ankle as (what I thought would be) the grand finale of my 50th birthday celebration. Little did I know. . .

May 16, 2007

Dear Katie,

When you unblock you REALLY unblock. I will try to answer some of your questions in this letter but some may come later. They not only aren't easy, they aren't simple either, as in 25 words or less.

First of all let me say that I hope your mom will not be too disturbed by my contacting you. My friend Gretchen, who gave me the first push on my search, is an adoptee also and her dad felt very threatened by her inquiries into her birth parents. I know from experience that there is more to being a mother than giving birth and I often feel that I do not legitimately have the right to consider myself your mother. Strange choice of words there I guess huh?

Now for the good news: Yes, I did give you a name. It was Melinda Louise. I recently obtained my hospital records and discovered that you were born at 7:51 p.m. You weighed 7 lbs (I knew that) and were 20 and 1/2 inches long. You had brown hair and blue eyes. You were one week overdue but didn't even leave a stretch mark.

I have indeed carried this secret all these years. When I decided to come out I discovered that my siblings have known for years but did not want to approach me about it. So much for secrets! I am writing an article that I hope to get published outlining the plight of birth mothers. "The Girls Who Went Away" (TGWWA) will give you many insights to our plight. I read the book early on in my search as it was recommended by other birth parents and adoptees. I am currently reading "Without A Map" by Meredith Hall, which also chronicles the hardship and shunning of a 16 year-old girl in a small town in New Hampshire.

It was only weeks ago that I "came out" to my children. And yes, Tim is one of them. For the most part their response was, "Oh Wow Mom! That is so exciting." And almost in the next breath, my California son asks: "Do you know who the father is?" I think I need to jerk that guy back here to Minnesota. He has obviously been in California too long.

I too, look forward to our meeting at some point so do not discard those pictures. When I finish this writing class I hope things settle down a little. I plan to have work done on my eyelids in June. They are interfering with my field of vision. I am also due for another colonoscopy as colon cancer is a concern in my family. I have not had it but do seem to grow the polyps that are precancerous. You might as well know also that I have rheumatoid arthritis but it is responding very well to medication and the only problem I have is some limitations in my right hand. I also fall down a lot but that is just clumsy and I don't think it is hereditary; too much gawking at the wonders of this world.

And OH MY GOSH, I still cannot tell left from right. On a good day I am lucky to know up from down. I have lazy eye (I am really in not very good shape now that I look at it) in my right eye so used to try to fake it that way. Then I got this wedding ring and thought that would help me keep things straight. When they say "right lane ends", it still throws me for a loop.

This experience has been traumatic for me in spite of the fact that I could see it coming. I can't imagine what it was like for you. I just want to push away from the world for awhile and wrap myself in this until it is absorbed. Everyone is so excited for me and I have a sister that is all over me about this and wanted to see pictures of your dogs. She is four years younger and always in my face. Has been since the day she was born.

I know you had important questions for me and I have no trouble answering them but do have to organize my thoughts and give you a satisfactory answer so *that will be coming. I hope that I have answered a few here and I am always open to more. You will no doubt be hearing more from me soon.*

Take care, Jackie

Dear Jackie,

    Thank you for taking the time to answer some of my questions for I am the Queen of questions! I completely understand you wanting to retreat and spend time absorbing all of the events of the past month and more I expect. I am at that place right now too. This week has been quite an experience and it's only Wednesday. My husband is going out of town for several days and I am looking forward to having the house to myself. I'm only sorry that I have so much going on this weekend that I won't be around to take full advantage of this rare opportunity for solitude.

    Take all the time you need to answer my other questions. I have been browsing through "The girls who went away" and have a whole new perspective on what you may be going through at this time. My concerns are fairly minimal compared to what could be going on in your head. Rest assured that I am a very safe person. I bear you no ill will, have no feelings of being rejected by you and look forward to seeing where all this leads us.

Take care, Katie

May 19, 2007

Dear Jackie,

I will be seeing my mom later this morning and will be sharing my news with her. I have had several days to contemplate my approach which, as seems to always be my way, will be open and direct. We will then have the opportunity to explore as much or as little as she is ready for. I have purchased a second copy of *TGWWA* to leave with her. I don't know if, or when, she will read it but since she is an avid reader, I expect at some point she will pick it up.

Your contacting me may inadvertently bring Mom and me closer together. I don't want to tell you too much about her at this time for several reasons. First and foremost, I suspect you have plenty on your plate without having to absorb more information about the woman who took on the role that you were denied. Secondly, I don't think it is appropriate to share that part of my life without her knowing about our reconnection. Perhaps one day you two will meet. You share common interests (aside from ME!) as she is a writer and bookworm too.

Anyway, if you have been concerned about me regarding this delicate task that I must complete, please know that I am in a very good place this morning and am actually looking forward to talking to her. I feel as though I have been taking care of everyone else these past few days and once I talk to Mom, I can start to take care of myself. Yes, I am the caretaker in our family and sometimes the universe it seems!

On a humorous note, I dropped my husband off at the airport just in the nick of time for I was about to choke him! He is so terribly fascinated by this process and understandably so, but there have been times when I just want to sit and think while he wants to talk and talk and talk. . . My stepson Todd, who is just like his dad, is so interested and supportive. I sent him our emails and he had to take a break after reading the 3rd one as he couldn't read through the tears. One day I will tell you all about Todd and our relationship; he is an awesome person with a wicked sense of humor. He asked me last night if I had heard any more from his new grandmother! Your California son sounds a lot like Todd and as they both reside on the west coast (Seattle) perhaps there IS something in the water out there.

I will close now as I suspect you have been trying to cocoon yourself away from the questions, excitement and concern of those who love you most. Take care and know that I will be fine.

Love, Katie

PS - Because my life just isn't quite exciting enough these days, I am going to look at a cat at the Humane Society this afternoon. He is a 1 year-old male, silver tabby shorthair with green eyes and weighs 14 lbs!! A big boy! I expect you are familiar with the events that can transpire when adding a new pet to the household and must think I am crazy! Hell, I think I must be crazy!!!! But if he passes my "purr test" it will be a done deal!

Oh Katie!

Good luck with your "errand" this morning. I know you will handle it well. And come out the other side unscathed. I know how you feel about just wanting to be quiet and sort things out for yourself. I hope you have a little solitude this week-end. It feeds the soul I find. As for me I am having a card club here today and so was going to use tomorrow afternoon to compose answers to some of your deeper questions. It sounds like your family is as curious about me as mine are about you. I think they don't realize that we must take things slowly to absorb it all. Your keeping me abreast of your progress displays a measure of trust I was not expecting so soon. Take care now.

Jackie

P.S. Just read your P.S. We are cat people here as well. We don't have our own but there are 8 among the 5 of them. One of my daughters has a 19 year old that is hanging in. They are such fun. I hope he is waiting for you.

Dear Jackie,

I just returned from the Humane Society and the cat is a grey tabby, not silver, so I will quite likely pass on him however it has gotten my "I need a kitten" juices flowing. At least that is cheaper than new car fever which I <u>always</u> succumb to!

My visit with Mom went extremely well. My intention had been to leave her with copies of our correspondences that she could read whenever she felt ready; she was ready within 10 minutes so Winston and I went for a walk around the block while she read them. We had a very good talk and, not to put you on the spot or anything, she is already looking forward to meeting you one day!!! Blew me away! As you know, I left her a copy of *TGWWA* and I expect she will be browsing through it before the day is over.

There are bound to be ups and downs for her as she goes through the process of adjusting to this information however, she wants me to keep her up-to-date as all of this unfolds. I have encouraged her to call if she thinks of any questions. (Is this beginning to feel like a fairy tale of sorts to you too?) Enjoy your cards this afternoon and I will look forward to hearing from you.

Katie

Birth and Surrender

Hi, Katie,

Now for one of the big questions: What was it like to give you up? I have written this letter in my head a dozen times so hope I get it right.

Let me start from the beginning briefly. I was born in St. Joseph's Hospital (coincidence?) in Mankato, Minnesota. I am the oldest of five and spent my formative years growing up in Mankato, LeSueur and Waseca. When I was fourteen, my dad died leaving my mother with five kids and not so much as two dimes to rub together as we used to say. I only mention this as it plays into one of my reasons for surrender. I graduated from high school in 1954 and soon thereafter took a job with Northwestern Bell Telephone Co. They paid $36 per week as opposed to the going rate of $30 for secretaries. Whee!

One year later Ma Bell was my ticket out of town when I transferred to Minneapolis. I soon took an apartment with 3 other girls. In the early part of 1956 I met your father. When I discovered I was pregnant I was ashamed but we were going to fix that by getting married. Right? Huh? By this time he was having second thoughts and it was an off again, on again, off again decision. Eventually we went to see one of the priests at St. Lawrence where I was attending Mass in those years. He referred me to a priest at St. Olaf, who tried to assure me that it was wiser to remain single, have the baby, and surrender the child than to marry someone who no longer loved me. I was still convinced that God and I could work this out.

The priest made an appointment for me to consult with a social worker at Catholic Charities and a program was set up for me. They gave me an alias, Joyce Jensen, and it was determined that when I could no longer hide my condition from Ma Bell, I would be taken to a work home. This was a family in Edina where I received room, board and $15 a week in exchange for housework and child care. Catholic Charities had also arranged an out of town address for me as I had told my mother that I was being transferred to Duluth. This was to somehow excuse myself from coming home for the holidays. I am a terrible liar though and could not bring myself to carry out the lie. So I called Mom. Of course she was shocked and disappointed; and worried about how to cover this shame from the neighbors, her relatives, and even from my siblings. Many times during the next months I had to console her and tell her that I felt everything was going to work out. And I believed that. During my prayers a feeling of peace would come over me that assured me that everything was going to be alright. What I didn't realize was that my idea of "alright" and God's were not the same.

Six weeks before my due date, which was March 27 by the way, I was transferred to the Infants Home on

Carroll Avenue in St. Paul. There were between 30 and 40 girls in residence ranging in age from 14 to 43. Another girl went in that same day and since the dorms were full, we were given temporary quarters on the third floor. It was a very small room. I think it was probably kind of like an attic up under the eaves. I don't think the room had windows but my roommate and I didn't care as it was more private and not as noisy as the dorms.

We never did get moved down to second floor and when my roommate delivered early, I had the "attic" to myself. I think they forgot I was up there but I didn't mind.

Early in the morning hours of April 3 I determined I was in labor. Finally!! The nun/nurse in residence checked me and another nun rode in the cab to the hospital that afternoon. It was about four o'clock when I was admitted. I was prepped and checked on periodically and finally taken into the delivery. As I mentioned you arrived at 7:51 p.m.

There was a room at the hospital reserved for girls from the home. A screen was kept across the doorway so passers-by would not discover us or recognize us. One of the nurses was careless about closing the curtain and when we complained we were greeted with an attitude of it was our own fault that we were there in the first place. Sounds like something from TGWWA. I did not get to hold you but could peer at you through the glass at certain hours when the visitors were not there. I did hold you on the way back to the home in the cab. As soon as we arrived you were whisked into the nursery.

The next day I went back to the apartment. I was under the understanding that I could visit you any time. I was to find that this was not correct. It didn't matter for the first two weeks as I spent the days and nights for the most part sleeping and crying. Never heard of post partum depression and I am sure that most of my physical and psychological problems stemmed from that. I was still dealing with what to do about your future. My mother had said that I could not bring you home and I wondered how the world would treat a child that her own family rejected. I also was no stranger to insecurity and scarcity and could not foist a life of the same on an innocent child. I would pay for my "sin" but could not expect my child to suffer unnecessarily. But I needed another look. So I called the home and they finally reluctantly agreed that I might visit. The visit was short and my last sight of you was of lying in the crib while the nurse/nun tended to your needs. You looked at me with those big blue eyes and I knew in that instant that I had to get you into a home and parents with loving arms available to you.

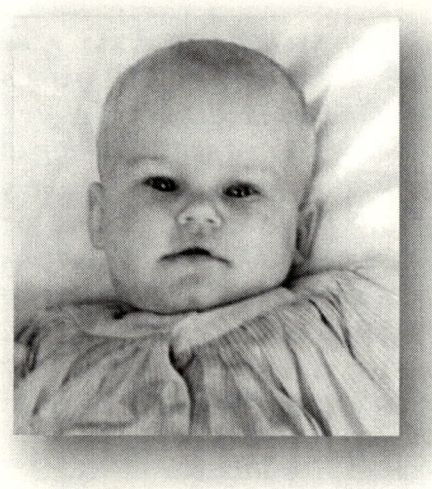

I recently received a transcript of some of the proceedings at the court house before the judge but I remember little but for the swearing part. When I left the court house I went directly home and cried one last cry and swore that nothing would ever touch me like that again. It was well over one year later that I discovered that I could picture you with your new family and not feel that awful resentment; a resentment born of grief and anger. Too bad we did not have support groups for women like me back then.

What I was feeling was no doubt natural but how was I to know? Who to talk to? Who to listen? My roommates soon found out that the subject was off limits. As I always do when I hurt, I want to be alone to sort it out. I cannot tolerate pity or sympathy for that matter. Kind of a stubborn streak there I guess but it works for me. And nature is a great healer.

So, I took back my name, went to work for the Star and Tribune, made new friends and made excuses when needed about those missing months in my life. If you have finished the book you know that some women never wanted to have another child after they surrendered their first born. I came under the heading of the other group, those looking for a replacement. (And I tried 5 times, please God.) But there is no such thing as a replacement I am finding out. There is always that empty place that kind of heals over but the experience becomes a part of the fabric of who we are. I concluded some years ago in my search for spiritual enlightenment that we come into this world with assignments. One of mine was to bear a child for someone who could not have one. And in so doing learn and grow to become the person I was meant to be. So there it is.

One last thing: In case you haven't noticed I have hardly mentioned your birth father. It is not that I can't or won't talk about him when and if you are ever ready. In fact I actually have much to thank him for but I have not seen him in almost 50 years and I bear him no ill will. I just wanted you to know that.

Love, Jackie

Hi, Katie,

I finished my letter and I hope you received it all right. It was three pages long and almost snailed it instead. I also hope I did not overdo some of the details. I am not sure exactly what you wanted but any questions I will be happy to answer.

It is quiet here this afternoon except for the TV. Bill is watching the Twins. He leaves on Saturday for a week in Romania. I don't know why but I seem to get more done when he is gone. Also I don't mind being alone for some time. At my age I have many friends who are alone due to losing a spouse and I know they must be very lonely at times. I remind myself of this when Bill gets on my nerves. I was talking to my instructor, who is 75, about crabbiness. We could never understand why old women are crabby. Now we are one of them and still don't know why.

So what is the kitty count at your house? You mentioned that you already had one cat right? Think I will go work on this week's lesson. Hoping to get your spin on the letter.

Love, Jackie

Dear Jackie,

Thank you so much for such a heartfelt letter. I can only imagine the memories that it must have brought up. As I sit here with tears streaming down my face, I hurt for you and the circumstances you found yourself in, in a time when women didn't have the choices that are available these days. And to find yourself with few people to talk to . . . heartbreaking at best. I don't say these words out of pity but straight from the heart, with a feeling of empathy and compassion.

I rejoice as well for perhaps the wound can begin to heal now that you have taken the brave first step of putting yourself out there to family, friends and perhaps the greatest risk of all, to me. And so far, so good eh! I will write more of my reactions to this special message a little later; I am feeling emotionally overwhelmed at this time and am fortunate to have been able to write this but I wanted you to know how much your letter has touched me.

Yes, I do have one cat already (Spook) and have not added to our household this weekend. When I got home from Mom's yesterday afternoon I made myself lie down on the couch with a good book and Winston to avoid an impulse kitten purchase.

Last night I went to my Dad's for a graduation party for a young relative and ended up having an opportunity to share my news with him. He was so thrilled and excited for me! One day soon I will share my life story with you and you will get to know and understand what my life has been like.

Speaking of fathers, I have not asked about my birth father because right now is about us. There will be time for that later. We need to take care of ourselves at this tender time in our relationship.

In closing I would like to say that I think you are a very brave, strong, caring and compassionate woman. Everyone who has read our correspondences makes several comments. First of all, they comment on how alike we sound and secondly, that you sound like a wonderful person whom they would like to meet. Several people also want to know if your laugh sounds like mine; I guess we'll have to wait and see about that.

Love, Katie

Dear Katie,

Thank you for responding to my letter. I was not sure how it would be received. I would indeed like to know a little about your life in the DeCosse household. I also wondered how the agency paired you with that family or was it just that their number came up. I like to think that they were very careful about how and where they placed you. I have a feeling that our voices are much the same for some reason.

It is hard to believe that one week ago we knew little of each other. Look how far we have come in such a short time. Amazing! I was afraid you might not respond in the first place or at least not as quickly. This has certainly been a week of emotional ups and downs.

Your Spooky cat looks a little like Tim's. He has two littermates named Felicity and Schrodinger. He majored in philosophy before going to law school. Guess that is where the names came from.

You also mentioned Todd in one of your letters. Now I am curious. It sounds like you have a good relationship with your extended family. I can kind of understand why. I am really looking forward to knowing more about you and how you got to where you are in this life. Plenty of time for that. Take care now.

Love, Jackie

Dear Jackie,

Yes, isn't email amazing!!! We have probably covered material that would have taken 6 months back in the day of the agency being the go-between. Some of your questions/inquiries are going to take some time to respond to and some I may not have answers to. I talked to Mom this AM and she told me several things that I never knew about my adoption story.

One interesting thing was that every time the agency called and said they had a baby, something else was going on in the DeCosse household. For instance, when they called and said my older brother was ready for placement, they had just (that same day) received the news that my dad's youngest brother had been killed in a car accident and they would need to travel to Bozeman, MT for the funeral. My mom had to wait another few days to pick up the baby she had been wanting for so long. And to have to put a mourning face on while inside she must have been so excited to know that she was finally going to have a baby. . . wow. When they received word that I was ready for placement, my dad's older brother was getting married in NY a week later and so she had to leave me almost immediately. The mother of my godmother came to take care of us and saw that I was hugged, snuggled and taken care of.

One thing I can talk about is Todd. He is the biological child of my husband and his first wife. He and Lynn are about 3 weeks apart in age. While Lynn and I have always had a special bond because we are both adoptees, she is much more reticent about sharing information. Todd is so much like his dad in that he wants to talk about everything.

I came into their lives when they were 9 and they are now 37. I have never intruded on their mother's role as "mom". We oftentimes refer to me as the Wicked Stepmother or Wicked Wanda; all in jest of course. I feel that I have had the best of both worlds. Todd and Lynn fill the spot of children for me and yet we don't have much "baggage". I have a very comfortable relationship with their mother and will, on occasion, receive doggy question phone calls from her.

Todd and I have always been very close. I think he looks to me for counsel that is unhindered by parental roles or expectations and I love him like a son. He is very bright but still hasn't quite figured out what he wants to do with his life. At this time he is devoting most of his energy to raising his daughter and I must say he is doing an incredible job.

Todd is so intrigued by our process and so thrilled for me/us. When I was talking to him this afternoon he said that perhaps I shouldn't mention that I am sharing our correspondences with others; he is afraid that you may decide to not share as much knowing that others are reading our emails. Does this bother you? In any event, that is an example of how Todd looks out for others, one of the things I love most about him. Another thing about him that I treasure is his sense of humor and wit. We laugh so hard sometimes we cry. He seems to think that you and I need to take a trip to Seattle so we have a chance to get to know each other without outside interference; a pretty transparent idea on his part.

You will hear more about him in the coming weeks, months, and years but that is Todd in a nutshell. I have started writing my life story for you but it will be a several day project as I am not sure where to begin and how much you want to know at this time. I don't know that anyone knows how carefully children are placed in their new homes; perhaps a number does just come up. I can certainly ask Mom about that. I know that they did go through the home study and application process but beyond that . . . .

Oh yikes, look at the time! My weekend is fast disappearing and what a weekend it has been!! Not as relaxing as I had hoped but oh so productive. Mom has simply amazed me in her acceptance of this event and the ones to come, and the rest of the family will follow her lead. I feel such relief and feel that I can proceed with our reconnection in whatever way feels right. Sleep well.

Love, Katie

May 21, 2007

Hi, Katie,

To address Todd's concerns about how much you should share I have to say, "What else is there?" I have committed the ultimate sin, 'fessed up and put a face on it. (No, you were not an immaculate conception. Sorry!) I have the impression that you are a very open person with an outgoing and dynamic personality where I am inclined to be reserved and introspective. I substitute high strung for dynamic. So I will let you censor anything that you think needs it. Does Todd ever come to the Twin Cities?

I have been thinking some about your mother and what it was like to get a phone call out of the blue and hear that your baby is here, come and get her. No nine months warning there I guess. I find this all a little surreal to say the least. I don't quite know what my boundaries are and do not want to overstep any of them. It is a strange spot to find myself in.

I have discovered in my spiritual journey that every time I think I have the answers, I discover I have more questions. One that keeps popping up is this: When I first contacted Catholic Charities a few months back, they told me that you had made an inquiry in 1979. Is that correct? People keep referring to that and I wonder if it is true. My son Tom had to take time off work to process that. Just think what it would have been like to have you in his life all of these years. Was he being greedy? Was he just thinking of himself? Yet what did he miss by not knowing you? Tom tends to be a little over-scrupulous. I thought that the two older sisters I gave him might have been a clue.

I must sit down and put the events of the last few months in chronological order as so much has happened so fast. I love your long letters and look forward to them. Have a good week.

Love, Jackie

Dear Jackie,

I intend to write a much longer message to you this evening but will answer your question about my inquiry in 1979. Yes, I did contact Catholic Charities in 1979 and requested any and all *non-identifying* information that was available and there was A LOT. I suspect that at some point you filled out a form listing family and relatives for yourself as well as my birth father. I had no intention of going any further at that time or since, unless you initiated the contact - which now you have!!

I find it extremely interesting that Tom had to take time off to process something I did almost 30 years ago and he hasn't even known of my existence for much more than 30 days! Kids - they ALWAYS surprise you don't they?

As an adopted child, the "story" included the supposition that you placed me for adoption to give me a better life and a better life for you too; essentially that you would go one way and I the other and never the two shall meet. (Very 1950's sounding!) So I never pursued a search, in part because I didn't want to disrupt the new life that you had made for yourself and that I was quite likely forgotten long ago.

Anyway, I will write more this evening especially in response to your story of my birth and surrender. I have decided to take tomorrow off from work as I don't have any classes to teach. I usually do my clinic site visits on Tuesday but will do those on Friday instead as we have that day off from school as well. As an aside, Camden will be one of my visits this week and I expect you know that they have just recently moved into their new building.

Love, Katie

Dear Jackie,

I have been composing this letter in my head all day long, one little snippet at a time. First of all, I'm glad you enjoy my long emails as this one will probably be quite lengthy. I have not known how much you want to hear about at this time but I sense that you are willing to read it all. I have discovered that I communicate best through writing especially when dealing with emotionally charged issues and they don't get much more charged than this! I find myself choking on my foot on a regular basis but when I write I can edit; not the feelings but the interpretation by the reader. I can say what I need to say and feel fairly certain that the message comes through as intended.

Perhaps I should start with Tom and why this is the best time for us to connect. My step-daughter Lynn searched and found her birth parents when she was in her early 20's. I don't want to share too much of her story for it is her story to tell but I did gain some insights into the entire process and I have said many times in the past week (has it only been a week since I read your first letter - hard to believe!) that I feel much better equipped to handle the emotional journey that this will be at 50 years of age than at 20 something, 30 something and even 40 something. I, like you, believe that everything happens for a reason in its own time.

Now back to Tom. Thirty years ago, your children would have been quite young and hardly equipped to handle the arrival of an older sibling who, from their perspective, might have been seen as an intruder. Also, 30 years ago, you had children to raise and all the time and various commitments that goes along with 5 different schedules. Now we are both less encumbered with responsibilities and can devote time to our own interests.

From what I have read in *TGWWA* about reunions, I get the impression that many times, once the novelty and initial excitement wears off, the new found relationship tends to dwindle to very little contact and the birth mother experiences the loss all over again. I don't want that to happen and 30 years ago that may indeed have been the result. I also know that I would not have the support and encouragement from my parents that I am so surprised and pleased to have now. It seems as though all the stars have lined up and now is the right time for us to meet and be able to maintain a relationship for the duration of our time on earth.

At 50 it is much easier to put the questions out there and to be able to share myself with an attitude of this is who I am and it is good enough. Yes, some may say that many years have been wasted but I choose to look at it as, "now we are able to make the most of this journey." While I try not to quote country music singers, one song has always meant a lot to me - Garth Brooks' "The Dance". One of the lines is, "I could have missed the pain, but I'd have had to miss the dance". I usually think of this when I suffer a loss. In our circumstances, the pain came first and now there is the dance. Let's make the most of it!

It's time to inject a little humor into this message. I emailed our correspondences to my niece, June, who is my sister Lucy's daughter. (The Lucy story is very long and complex and one that can wait.) June is 26 years old and pregnant with her first child. She left me a message this afternoon that cracked me up. Her words were: "Wow Katie! That is so exciting. I don't know what to say except 'holy crap!' "She is a very good writer and I love her emails however this is something she wants to talk about over the phone as she doesn't even know where to begin with her questions and comments.

Yes, Todd does come to the Twin Cities on occasion but due to money constraints, it is not nearly often enough so Don and I usually travel to Seattle at least once or twice a year to visit there. Todd and Liberty (his daughter) were here this spring for my big 50th birthday bash. When the time comes and you to be ready to meet him, I will gladly purchase a plane ticket for him. Who knows, he may already have his bag packed as he is that excited about this.

Your letter of yesterday afternoon regarding my birth and surrender is so beautifully written and heart-wrenching. I am trying to avoid feelings of having to be worth the pain you went through in carrying me and then through the ultimate act of love, giving me up so that I could have the chance at a better life than you felt you could provide for me. These feelings are self-inflicted and are by no means a reflection of any expectations that I feel you have put on me. They come from the part of me that feels that I must be worthy of the love and affection of others. As you can see, I am still a work in progress!

And your last image of me - very powerful. I am so looking forward to sharing my pictures with you but have gathered from reading *TGWWA* that this may be a very delicate experience for you. You will need to let me know when you are ready to see them. I don't have them on the computer so we will have to look at them together in person. I must say I was pretty cute!

I'm not sure what you want to hear about regarding the intervening 50 years since we were last together. It is not a fairy tale by any means but it is the experience that has made me the person I am today and for that I wouldn't change a minute of it.

By now you may have gathered that my parents are divorced and have been for 26 years. My father in fact, is today celebrating his 24th wedding anniversary to his second wife, Paula. I have never been particularly close to my father but have always been proud to be his daughter. Few people would argue the fact that he is a creative genius. His business acumen and creativity has been likened by some to that of Walt Disney. That creative drive does not lend itself to being a very present and active "dad". He was also raised in a time when the father's role was to provide for the family and he did that; we never went without food, clothing, shelter or education. He and Mom instilled in us the values of working for the extras so, although I was raised in a fairly affluent neighborhood, we were not just handed the extras. We had to earn those and as most children would, felt that we were deprived when compared to the neighbors who simply handed over the boats and cars etc. In hindsight, I am glad of that for it made me appreciate the value of working towards goals.

My mother had a difficult life being married to someone so invested in his own talents and ideas. At this time she is a recovering alcoholic with 27 years of sobriety under her belt. I was instrumental in starting the intervention process, one of my life changing events. I am proud to say that she has worked hard over the years to make changes in her life and no longer is the person that I grew up with. She feels an enormous amount of guilt about the years that can never be relived. My fondest hope is that one day she will forgive herself and let it go. We were never physically neglected as her drinking did not take her out of the home but there was definitely emotional neglect. I have forgiven her; now she must forgive herself.

I think you will enjoy meeting her one day. My husband never knew her in her drinking days and is unable to imagine the dichotomy between the person he knows and the person I describe in my childhood. She, like my father, is extremely bright and artistic but much more down to earth.

I am not sure exactly what you meant by boundaries and would appreciate some clarification on that.

Anything I write to you can be shared freely with anyone you choose. And I hope you are sharing our letters with others. Secrets suck! And you have lived with such a huge one for so long that I hope you are feeling freed these days - I know I would! Take care and I so look forward to your response to this loooooooooooong email. I have a feeling that our first face to face meeting will be sooner rather than later!!?!!

Love, Katie

PS - I did manage to get tomorrow off. Please tell Tom that I look forward to meeting him someday soon and he will be very glad that he didn't have to put up with me for the past 30 years!!

Hi, Katie,

Thank you for your long letter. There are so many similarities in the way you were raised and the values we instilled in our children. My husband and I are both thrifty and careful and do not believe indulging for the sake of indulgence. Our children learned early the value of earning their own buck. Also my husband had a drinking problem when the children were growing up and I often felt like a single parent. I too have a lot of guilt but think that goes with the territory. I don't think I would ever win a Mother of the Year award but happily my children grew to be self sufficient adults and if they aren't happy, I guess that is something they will have to take care of. I always think I was lucky that they came with such good stuff and that made up for my deficiencies. When I address this concern with my youngest, Joe, he says "Mom, you were a 'scholar' raising five kids". Joe is into life progressions and apparently he excuses me.

As to the information you received, I think someone talked to your father but I didn't realize to what extent. I wasn't there at the time. One thing I didn't know at the time was that there is a smidgeon left of Native American blood from my mother's side of the family. We just can't agree what tribe we "belong" to but I think it is Cree.

As to the boundary question, though I gave birth to you I know there is more to being a mother than giving birth and yet at some level the intervening years disappear in my mind and it is just you and me again and I don't want to overlook the 50 years that came between nor step on the toes of those who deserve the title they worked so hard to earn. I hope I put that delicately enough.

You were so right on in understanding how this would have played out in the years when my kids were young. I was overwhelmed with my duties and after seeing how absorbed I have been this past week, (today I tried to put the jar of mayo in the garage), and I can't imagine how I would have dealt 30 years ago.

I have been sharing some of your letters and pictures but first I need to be a little stingy. This has been mine for so long that I am reluctant to let go. Now that is just silly.

I will pass your message on to Tom and I look forward to meeting as it seems there are so many things left to discuss but I have to let you orches-

trate this journey as that is only fair since I am the instigator. OK?

Love, Jackie

May 22, 2007

Dear Jackie,

As is typical for me, even on my days off I am up at the crack of dawn. As I write this I have already been up for an hour. That's one thing I love about email; I can "talk" anytime I want. It is especially useful when contacting students who probably don't want to hear my bright cheery voice at 6 AM!!

I am looking forward to sharing your recent emails with my mom. She too often felt like she was a single mom and those are her exact words! I know that she feels very vulnerable to you in the area of her alcoholism and yet, that was a part of your life in the intervening years as well. Joe's comment about you being a scholar raising children would be a very apt description of her too. My mother is 78 and so both of you raised children in the same environment of social mores and expectations of what a "good" marriage and family were "supposed" to be.

We seem to be tiptoeing around the topic of our first face to face meeting; who instigates it, and when, and where, etc. You have acknowledged that you are more reserved while I am at a time in my life where I say "Bring it on!" to just about everything. Perhaps if we explored our expectations and "ground rules" we can come to a mutual decision on this. We have covered so much territory in the past 8 days (!) that I feel that I am ready to take this step at any time. I would rather skip the talking by phone bit as I want to see and hear you for the first time, at the same time. After reading what I will now refer as "the book" I know that there is bound to be a process once we do meet and I feel well equipped to handle whatever comes later.

I picture us meeting somewhere beautiful, colorful and somewhat private and will come armed with a box of tissues. I think that if we can agree to be totally honest about things like needing a little space at times as we travel on this journey, everything will be fine. I have no expectations of you and I mean that in a good way. Give what you can, when you can and know that it is all good. At this time in my life, I am not looking for another "mom" but rather an enduring relationship with the woman who gave birth to me and I suspect never stopped loving me. I already feel an enormous connection to you that will one day truly be called love.

I look forward to meeting your children and there too, I see that connection as being very fun and yet I hope it is not threatening to them, especially your daughters, whom by the way, you have spoken of very little. :) What do they think? Please reassure them, if necessary, that I do not see myself as taking their place in your heart. I just want to meet them and see where that goes. I have always wanted sisters, however, I have no expectations of them needing to fill that hole in my life; if it happens, great! If not, no harm done.

I have a few other questions for you. You haven't said much about your husband and as I have worked for years with veterinarians, I have a pretty good idea of what he is like. However, I am curious as to whether your "secret" has been kept from him all these years as well. I am also interested in knowing a little bit about your search for me. What obstacles fell away? How long did it take to find me? How did you get my name and then track me down? I am also interested in knowing how old your children are these days; obviously all younger than I but by how much? I suspect that one or more of them is about as old as my stepchildren.

In one of my emails I said that I was a very safe person and several people have asked me what I meant by that and perhaps you wonder too. In writing that I meant that I am very non-judgmental, always willing to give people the benefit of the doubt; I am empathetic and very trustworthy. I once asked my students to tell me what they felt was their best trait as a person and as is my way, I too answered that question. My response was and is, "I am a very good friend. I will go the wall for the people I care about!"

One other thing I am very interested in but this can wait, is your menopause experience for they say that the best indicator of how it will go, is knowing the experience of one's mother. Several years ago I was in a very dark place and easily given to crying. I went to the Dr. who prescribed antidepressants which I prefer to call my "happy pills" and that has made such a difference. He prescribed one that also helps with hot flashes and as long as I avoid too much caffeine, I do notice a difference. I still am plagued by hot flashes but always carry a fan in my purse and know how to use it!

I know you have talked about taking this slowly and will now put the ball back in your court. I am ready at any time so let me know your thoughts.

I have attached a picture of me at about age 2. It is my favorite picture of me as a child and I think you will enjoy it. *(See back cover)* I had never seen it until about 7 years ago. I am sending you a photo of the photo and so there is some background glare but I think you can still see enough of it to enjoy it. I have indeed framed it and it is BIG - 13 x 19! I know that once you see the other pictures of me, my dad would be happy to reprint any that you would like to keep copies of.

Katie

Dear Jackie,

I just had a long conversation with Mom and do have some answers regarding my placement in the DeCosse family. As part of the application process they had to have 3 letters of recommendation. Mom asked one of the nuns at St. Kate's to write one of them. This nun was, unbeknownst to Mom, the director of religious something or other at Catholic Charities. Because of this, my parents were quite likely given preferential treatment when it came to placements of children.

Also as part of the process, Mom and Dad had to fill out a form describing what they were looking for in a child. Things such as eye color, nationality etc. because lord knows, you didn't want to place a blue-eyed baby with two brown-eyed parents!! My parents felt that these things were not important however, they explained that they were going to be in a position to provide a college education to their children and would like a child that would have the potential to take advantage of that opportunity. The information that you and my birth father were "of superior intelligence" and an "A-grade average" respectively, were probably the overriding reasons for my placement with the DeCosse's. So you see, at least in my case, they were quite discerning in their placement of me.

Mom has shared some other stories that I had never heard before and one day I will share more of this with you. One funny story she reminded me of was that the day I was brought to their home, the dog ran away to my grandma's house which was not far away. We always thought that he wasn't that crazy about the change in his status when my brother came along and when I showed up, he was "out of there" as they say! He eventually came home and stayed but his nose was out of joint for awhile! I look forward to your responses to these 3 emails; I guess that once I get going it is hard to stop.

Love, Katie

Hi, Katie,

Oooh precious! You know, I have a picture of Anne at about that age and she looks much like you. I will try to find it. Meanwhile I am forwarding this to my sister. She is such a hound for any info on you that I have to beat her off with a stick but I will give her a treat today.

As to our meeting now, Sunday afternoon would be good for me if that works for you. I have to have Bill at the airport about noon on Saturday so after that would work also. He said we can meet while he is gone. (Like he would be invited?) I don't know what venue meets your criteria since I have never needed one for this purpose before. I always like Baker's Square but don't think that is intimate enough. Anyplace in Maple Grove is good. Houlihan's is kind of quiet and comfy. What think you?

I am going to write more later as you have given me a lot to sort out and answer. I need to get away from the house for awhile so will run a few errands. I find that getting behind the wheel is very therapeutic. Turn up the country station and sing-along.

Love, Jackie

Dear Jackie,

I am so glad you liked the picture. It is interesting that several times over the years people have commented that they know of someone who looks a lot like me and with more conviction than simply a vague similarity. One person in particular was a teacher of mine who also taught at the University of Minnesota and was referring to a student. One of your daughters perhaps?!!

Yes, let's meet on Sunday afternoon. This idea of mine is certainly negotiable but I would like to meet first at a park and then go to lunch. I expect that our first sighting of each other will be rather emotionally charged and as I tend to cry at the drop of a hat (AT&T commercials have been known to bring on the tears!), I would rather do that in a place where others don't have to bear witness to my emotions. Then we can dine and talk, and talk, and talk. . . Houlihan's sounds like a good idea and is rather private and subdued. Great plan on your part. Let me know what you think about the park idea as I am not married to it so to speak; I just think it would help me. If it is raining that day, we may have to go to plan B.

I just got off the phone with a very dear friend of mine from college. She has always been interested in my status as an adoptee and when she found herself unable to have children, I was a good sounding board for her as she went through the steps of adopting her son. Anyway, I have forwarded all our email to her and she has asked if she can share them with her adoption support group which of course I readily encouraged her to do. So it seems as though our reconnection may have far reaching effects on a lot of people; people we don't even know but who will treasure the beauty of what we have been able to share in such a short amount of time.

Love, Katie

PS - And you like country music too; isn't that a kick in the head. Although he is not always politically correct, Toby Keith is one of my all time favorites. I just can't seem to get enough of that voice.

The Search

Hi, Katie,

I think I will start with the "search" as it might get kind of long. I need to back up a little. Bill and I were married in 1961. Before we married I told him about you and then said I never wanted to speak of it again. He honored this request, though it must have been on his mind. About 10 years ago he brought it up and said if I ever wanted to find you he would help all he could. I was in a bad place at the time so I kind of blew it off.

Many times I had thought about you over the years and wondered if you would try to contact me. I thought all YOU had to do was go to the agency and get my info. That is how ignorant I was. I set little benchmarks for myself. I am a combination procrastinator and queen of denial. I told myself that when my mother passed away I would try. She died in '91 and I was going to North Hennepin Community College at the time. When I graduated I went to work to help the kids with tuition and living expenses until they got established.

We moved to Brooklyn Park in 2000 and Bill was involved in a business that was in trouble and it nearly put both of us away. Then I turned 70. I had to finally admit I was old. It was very traumatic as no birthday has ever been. We all know what comes after "old". One time I went online hoping to get some idea of how to go about searching. I don't think it occurred to me to check with the agency so I put it on the back burner again. Then last fall I ran onto a letter in the Catholic Spirit from an adoptee, Gretchen Traylor, who is involved in getting the rules changed for adoptees. I thought maybe this lady could give me a clue. So I gave her a call. Of all the places in the diocese that she might have lived, it turned out she lives about a mile from me.

Gretchen told me to call the agency and get an affidavit of disclosure and file it with the state and the agency would get a copy. This I did and was told I could also put a letter in your file. Which I did. (It was kinda dumb. I hope you never ask for it.) It was at that time that they told me you had inquired in '79 but couldn't tell me much else without a check to cover it.

One day Gretchen called and asked if I wanted to go to a Minnesota Coalition for Adoption Reform (MCAR) meeting. They like to get us "old" birth mothers involved. At the meeting I ran into a searcher who gave us some clues as to how to look up birth certificates etc. I had not decided to search but just be available. If there is one thing I have found about adoptees and mothers, birth or otherwise, is that they love a challenge. Throw them a bone and they don't stop until they have the whole dog. They have to get all the pieces of the puzzle in place. Connect all the dots and before I knew it this thing had taken on a life of its own.

I had told Bill that I was putting my info out and right away he thinks we should search regardless of cost. We operate differently. He is pushy whereas I like to let things play out. Anyway I did go to one of my sisters who I knew was aware of you and asked her exactly who knew. She replied: "Oh everybody". They had been tiptoeing around that elephant in the living room all these years, not wanting to voice their questions for fear of hurting my feelings. Now it was out in the open and were there ever questions.

Now back to the search. Gretchen said that when the weather warmed, (this was January) she would go with me to search for birth records. She finally reached someone who gave her the names of all of the girls born in Ramsey County on that day. We arranged to meet in order to sift through twenty names to find out which was you.

Before that came about I went to Concerned United Birthparents (CUB) meeting with Gretchen. She hadn't been in some years as she did not like driving that far alone at night and since I lived so close... See what was going on here? Doors were popping open right and left. At the meeting I was encouraged to tell my story and afterward a private searcher, Marj, approached me and asked my maiden name. She said she would like to try finding my child.

A day later she called with the names, the same ones that Gretchen had and more. I don't know the secrets of the trade but she was phenomenal. She not only had the names but the parent's names and how many children in the family and their ages. The one clue we had, and this is fantastic, is that when you were placed in the home, the social worker told me that the family had a little boy about 2 years old running around. So, we needed to find a family with a son born in '55. That narrowed the search to 2. So, Gretchen and I trucked to St. Paul to get birth certificates, the revised kind available to adoptees. I took them home and called Marj. When I described the documents to her, Marj said, "They are both adopted". And she described both of you. The other lady had green eyes and that almost ruled her out. I said that I wished I could see pictures. After some hesitation, Marj said she could fix that. She also got addresses. We soon ruled out the green eyed lady.

But I still had a dot to connect. I needed to know beyond a doubt that we had the right person. So she was able to find records, I don't know how she does this, and came back and said that Melinda was indeed Katie. She also was able to tell me that the house on Cleveland was owned by one Donald Prieb but didn't know what his connection was with you. (I thank God that you still maintain your maiden name.)

I thought that perhaps when you turned 50 you would check with the agency again if indeed you ever did. I thought you might call which you never did. So I composed a letter and wanted to get it to you after Mother's Day. In order to verify your address I asked Tim to call from his office. He got back to me with a positive address. On Saturday morning I mailed the letter about 10:30 a.m. I mentally followed that letter all week-end, from the post office in Brooklyn Park to downtown Minneapolis. Monday morning I pictured it at your station and being sorted and picked up by your mailman. By mid-afternoon I thought it was probably in your mail box.

I thought you would be home by five and picking up your mail. I thought you might call. If you didn't *call by 8 maybe you hadn't gotten the letter yet or weren't going to respond. Then I gave you until 9. Marj had said to give you time to absorb and decide whether you wanted contact. I went to bed fearful that I would be dogging the postman's steps, haunting my e-mail or jumping every time the phone rang until I heard from you. And the rest is history.*

Things just moved along so beautifully with little effort from me. People were put in my path to move this along. At last God and I seemed to be on the same page.

The day I told my children about it, I was driving back to Brooklyn Park and I had such an empty feeling in my gut. I needed a piece of pie or a turtle sundae or something. It was so strange. I managed to get home without stopping but I wonder what that was all about. So strange.

I am gradually opening up to my friends, one at a time. I guess I have hung onto it for so long that I can't part with it totally. It is a part of me. Maybe that is where that gut feeling comes from.

So there you have it. Maybe more than you wanted to know. I do appreciate that you told me what you learned from your mother about your placement. I am glad they took such good care to find a good home for you. I was amused at your dog story about how he left home when you arrived. We had a short haired dachshund when our kids were born. Conversely he was always curious about the new baby; sniffing and so on. He was very good with the children. If they pulled his ears, and he had good ears for pulling, he would just cry until he got our attention. Then when the child turned about a year and a half he would growl a little when they sat or laid on him. Like they should know he didn't put up with that anymore. Looking forward to Sunday.

Love, Jackie

Dear Jackie,

Thank you for the lengthy story of your search for me. And isn't it fortuitous that I did not change my maiden name. I haven't shared the Don story with you and must get to that soon as he is feeling rather neglected; it seems that the older he gets, the more everything becomes all about him! I give him crap about that all the time so we are able to laugh about it. When he gets too out there, a friend of mine has been known to step in and say, "Don, this is so not about you". As I recall we were talking about menopause and hot flashes at the time! But again, I digress. .

I didn't change my last name because at that time in my life I was very active in the Veterinary Technician profession on a national level. Many people had known me for a long time as Katie DeCosse and I was reluctant to lose my identity or create confusion for people looking for me - an odd choice of words but very apt! So Katie DeCosse I will always be.

I am glad that you were able to find people to assist you in your search for me. I expect the internet has helped many people connect and has sped up the process considerably. Time for me to toddle off to bed. Don has talked my ears into bloody stumps and I must return to the working world tomorrow morning. I am so glad I took today off as I probably wouldn't have accomplished a thing.

I too, am looking forward to Sunday and will see you at 1 PM. Please keep the emails coming in the meantime as I am so enjoying our correspondences.

Love, Katie

PS - I have shared our emails with a friend who has 2 children whom she adopted from Korea. Over the years we have talked at length about adoption and I know that this has helped her. I can't believe that I have known them since they arrived and one is out of college just this Spring and the other is one year out of high school. She was so touched and moved by our messages.

PSS - Just this evening I was looking around the house for pictures that I want to bring to show you; not just of me but of all my family. I expect it will be a good size bag of pictures. Fortunately I do have an 8 x 10 of the Easter dress picture so will leave the 13 x 19 at home on the wall.

May 23, 2007

Hi, Katie,

I drove by the park this morning after golf and the sign says Brooklyn Park Community Center or some such. You will see the white pagoda out front and I noticed a little pond as well. I "came out" to a good friend after we played golf and she is so excited. I am doing this gradually and it feels good. Some friends are just too good to be kept in the dark. Her name is Katie also and I gave her goose bumps.

You asked about my family. As you know we have five children. They are Anne, Margaret, Thomas, Timothy and Joseph, all born in a 7 1/2 year time period during the late 60's and early 70's. In 2000, Anne married Patrick Westen.

I have to say we lucked out with them. For the most part they are healthy although Tom had a brain tumor removed in 2001. I think there was only one speeding ticket in the whole bunch. At least that I know of. They minded their curfews and never came home drunk. I think if nothing else we did instill a sense of integrity in all of them.

At some point I am sure religion/spirituality will come up in our conversations. Let me just say this. About 18 years ago I woke to find myself experiencing *the dark night of the soul. It left me somewhat alienated from my religion. I even wrote an essay about it if you ever want to know more. Suffice to say that my spiritual journey has had me looking in other directions to enhance my relationship with the Creator or as I sometimes call Him, the "Maker of the Plan".*

So I think I have answered some of your questions. I still have to address the 'pause concern and will do that soon.

Jackie

Dear Jackie,

Thank you for the scoop on each of your kids; I see that several are close in age to Todd and Lynn which could be great fun! I will pour over these details more once I get home but wanted to thank you for bringing up the religion piece as I was concerned about that. I would love to read your essay!!! Briefly, I have little time for the Catholic Church these days; I used to be a C&E (Christmas and Easter) Catholic and am now just barely a W&F (weddings and funerals). I think it would be interesting to talk about this further; but essentially I find the church to be hypocritical at BEST and extremely discriminatory against women - those are my 2 biggies anyway. And yet I consider myself to be a spiritual person who tries to live by the "golden rule" and think it would be very interesting to explore this further together.

Katie

Dear Jackie,

   I don't know if I have the energy to write my usual long emails but we'll see how this goes. I was going to ask you if the park is on the right or left side of the street but recall that that is pointless; are you better at north vs. south side of the street? Not to worry, I will find it! I am familiar with the area and can always turn around if I miss it on the first pass. I am afraid that your pride in the number of speeding tickets your children have received is about to take a dive; I have 3 under my belt! At least I avoided getting them all within a year for it would be difficult to make my clinic visits from public transit! And those buggers are expensive! My insurance carrier has not discovered the evil of my ways and my rates have actually gone down! By the way I drive a blue/grey 2004 Honda Pilot. I have chuckled to myself several times when it occurred to me that you may have tracked me down through marriage licenses; speeding tickets would have been faster!!

   I loved hearing about your children; they sound like my kind of people. (Odd choice of words perhaps but fitting) I loved seeing Tom's picture and interview answers but am happy to say at this point that I don't look a thing like him! Please bring pictures of all of them if you are able and your husband too of course because I suspect that, while I don't think I have ever met him, his face may be familiar from various MVMA conferences. I have been to most of them in the last 25 years. I look forward to meeting them when we are all ready.

   Now I would like to share a little bit about Don and the history of our relationship. I met him when I was doing my senior Social Work internship at Hennepin County Medical Center (HCMC). At the time I was engaged to be married that summer right after graduation. Once Don and I discovered an attraction to each other I knew that I had no business marrying if I had such strong feelings for another so I broke off the engagement. Once I was done with my internship and the ethical issues had been removed, we began to build our relationship. We dated for about 4 years during which time I returned to school to pursue a degree in Veterinary Technology. Shortly after graduating from the Medical Institute of Minnesota, I moved in with him and we lived together for 14 years before getting married.

There were several reasons for this long period of time. First of all, I didn't think I wanted to ever have children but know enough about how that can change with age that I was reluctant to marry someone who most definitely did not want any more children. As Todd and Lynn reached college age, financial aid became an issue, especially for Lynn as graduate school was part of her plan. Her aid package would be based on family income and if we were married, my income would be considered and would reduce the amount of aid for which she was eligible. And lastly, like many couples who live together, we never seemed to get around to it! Finally on March 1, 1997 we did get married, one month before my 40th birthday. And yes, this year was our 10th anniversary followed shortly thereafter by my 50th birthday. It has been a very busy spring to say the least!

Back to Don for this is *supposed* to be about him! Don continued to work at HCMC, periodically moving from one department to another. He eventually worked on the psych ward and one of his responsibilities was to do all the suicide consults. One of the highest compliments ever paid to him came from the Chief of Psych. He commented that in all the years (7 I believe) that Don took care of this responsibility, he was never wrong in his assessment and evaluation of patients who had attempted suicide. Those who could safely be discharged were, and those who needed to be admitted were prevented from having the opportunity to "try again". Very high praise indeed.

Don retired from the county in 1999. In May of 2000 he was diagnosed with heart disease and underwent triple bypass surgery in July of that summer. While in surgery they discovered an aortic aneurysm and repaired that at the same time. He was in surgery for a very long 8 hours and remained in the hospital for about 10 days. His recovery was long but eventually he was back to his old self again. This was a very scary time for me as well as his children. Todd and Lynn were both living out of state at the time so there were many long phone calls between the 3 of us during those early days and weeks of recovery. They both were able to come home to see him and that was an enormous comfort to me.

For the most part, our years together have been peaceful, relaxed and lots of fun, ruled by mutual respect, support and love for each other. Due to the difference in ages, we have always been a rather unorthodox appearing couple; many people have made the assumption that we are father/daughter and the fact that I have always appeared younger than my age has not helped!!!! I recall one time when Don was shopping for a new vehicle and the salesman asked me what my dad thought of the truck. I told him that I didn't know as he wasn't here! I got used to the looks and assumptions and eventually stopped even noticing. Those people who are dear to us don't much care about the age difference and the rest don't matter. I must admit that it took my parents awhile to come around but eventually that happened too.

Until I came along, Don was not a pet owner with the exception of a couple gerbils who are now long gone. You must remind me to tell you the story of Todd and the gerbil. I introduced cats to his life and eventually a dog. That's a funny story too. Anyway, I will have time to share more of my life with Don and know that one day you will meet him for yourself.

So much for not having the energy to write a long email!!!! I must say that our email correspondences are provoking some very interesting comments and perhaps you are hearing these too. Todd thinks it should be published and he is not the only person to make that remark; almost everyone comments on how similar our writing styles and sense of humor are; several people have laughed through their tears and everyone has been touched by them in some way. You commented that your friend Katie had goose bumps after hearing your story; Sally, a coworker and dear friend, comes to my office every time she reads a new message just to show me her goose bumps!!

Once again it is time to head to bed; I am exhausted! How about you? Up until last night I was sleeping very well. I think that the anticipation of our meeting, mixed with a little apprehension as would be expected, is interfering with my sleep but I will have time to catch up on that later if need be.

Love, Katie

May 24, 2007

Dear Katie,

I woke at 4:00 and couldn't get back to sleep so you will excuse any errors in spelling and punctuation. I of course went to your letter right away. That Donald sounds like an OK guy. I am looking forward to meeting him.

One question that keeps coming to mind is what led you to become a Vet Tech? You asked about my husband so I will try to boil it down a little. Bill was raised on a farm in Beardsley, Minnesota which is located in that little hump on the back of the state. After high school he volunteered for the draft in order to qualify for the GI Bill. He enrolled at Iowa State University for pre-Veterinary and Veterinary Medicine. We were married 6 months before he graduated. He then was invited to intern at Angell Memorial Animal Hospital (ever heard of it?) in Boston so we spent 15 months in the east before returning to Minnesota.

He worked in several clinics here before opening Brooklyn Park Pet Hospital and ultimately Camden Pet Hospital. For 25 years he developed and oversaw the animal care department at the Humane Society. In the late eighties he became acquainted with the plight and conditions of the veterinarians in Cuba. The information they were working with was several years outdated. He then went to the University of Minnesota and downloaded the current technology and took that along with used computers to the institutes in Havana. He made several trips to Cuba and twice I went along. (I hope it is too late to get arrested.) Many times he traveled with the Pastors for Peace. I was not able to go on those trips because I do not have the necessary herd instincts and that would have put me away. In '94 he retired from practice.

I had shared a couple of our first letters with him. Then one day he asked if he could read the others. I handed him the book and later that day I caught him reading them a second time. He said he would understand if there was something I did not want him to read but so far that has not happened. Now he just asks if I have anything new for him to read and he makes sure I have them in chronological order. I am a very private person and he is a very nosey person and that is maybe why I am a very private person. If I am not careful he will take over and I can't have that.

Now as to you looking younger than your age, you get that from me. My sister always complains that I got the good genes but then I was here first. I also got the fat genes.

Back to the religion thing (don't get me started). I can surely empathize with your impatience at how the women are treated. A lot of it can be blamed on that St. Augustine dude who should be de-sainted. Don't know how he got in in the first place. By the way, did I mention that Joe is gay? So I have my own issues as well. I know that God loves him anyway and who am I to argue with God? I do still attend weekly Mass out of habit I guess and for Bill's sake as well.

Have you ever heard of Caroline Myss? I have been studying her take on spirituality. She is a medical intuitive and spiritual director. Raised in the church she has a Doctorate in theology and is now Episcopalian I believe. She still loves some things about the church but has lost faith in the hierarchy and understands that we do not have the whole truth, nor does anyone else. I heard her speak in Vegas a few years ago and find that I can accept and do believe many of the same things she teaches.

As to my kids, Anne adheres to the faith in which she was raised. I believe all of the others are dealing with their spirituality in their own way and I have come to accept that we have to do that. I have a very diverse family.

Now for Sunday: The community center will be on the north side of the street along with city hall and the police department. It is about half a block east of Zane. And I will definitely bring pix. You know, that sleep thing sounds good. Take care.

Love, Jackie

Dear Jackie,

I too was awake at 4 but managed to stay in bed until 5; I don't believe that it helps me feel more alert but I think I hold out hope that I will drift off again. I could probably get more accomplished if I just got up but 5:00 seems plenty early to start the day.

I will write more later but wanted you to know that I enjoyed reading your essay. Thank you for sharing the fact that Joe is gay. Their treatment of gays is another reason why I have parted ways with the Catholic Church. Oh, we are going to have so much to talk about!! I think we will have to meet more than once!! This morning I was listening to Toby Keith in the car and decided that at times, rather than being a Catholic, I am a Keithlic! I tend to feed my soul in a variety of different ways.

Until later, Katie

Dear Jackie,

Ah, it appears as though Bill is as fascinated as Don about our correspondences and upcoming meeting. Don too, likes to re-read them.

How did I land in the field of veterinary technology? First of all, I have always loved animals, dogs in particular but I have come to be a serious cat lover too and have had 7 in the past 24 years. I remember the dog we had when I was in high school and he was my dearest friend and confidant.

When I was a junior in college, I read the James Herriott books and seriously considered changing my major from Social Work to pre-vet. The thought of all that chemistry, biology and physics made me realize that this was a stupid plan and so I continued in my Social Work track. I have mentioned the politics of the time and being unable to find a job, so I took a position as a secretary - YIKES!! From there they moved me into sales which I grew to H-A-T-E. It was so bad that I would find myself crying on Monday morning when I was looking at another week of this horrible job. In October of 1981, I took a week off and saw an ad on TV for a veterinary technology program in the metro area. That reawakened my interest in working with animals and within 2 days I was registered to start in January 1982. I graduated in March of 1983 and worked as a clinic tech for 16.5 years. If you know anything about the profession, and I'm sure you do, that is about twice as long as most techs last.

I loved my job, loved the clients and was a fabulous tech if I may so myself! After 7 years I needed a change and went to work for Dr. John Lillie at Keller Lake Animal Hospital. I thrived there for many years but eventually burned out altogether. During my years as a vet tech I had a lot of great experiences. I was very active in our state association including serving as President. After that I also served on the national association and eventually was President of that too. I also had the opportunity to serve on the Wellness Committee of the AVMA and attended 2 meetings a year for about 7-8 years. I enjoyed all of this and met many wonderful people (oh dear, I'm sounding like a beauty queen!), some of whom have become life-long friends.

After I burned out, I took some time off and did . . . . nothing for about 6 months. It was great! I was able to read many books, spend time with friends and treasure Sunday nights because they were no longer a work night. In March of 2000 I took a job at Linder's Garden Center and had a ball!! It was so nice to punch in and punch out without having to worry about any animals. It was also such a beautiful place to work; lots of color, flowers and warm moist heat in the winter. Finally the heat of the greenhouse got to be too much to tolerate and I quit.

Shortly thereafter, a friend of mine called and said there was a veterinary technology teaching position available at a local college. She had given them my name because she thought I would be a great teacher. I'm glad she thought so because I was scared to death! Don too, had been saying for years that I should at least give it a try. So I applied, got the job and figured that if I didn't like it, I could quit after one quarter. And the rest is history. In January of 2005 I took on the role of Clinical Training Coordinator which involves placing students at internship sites. I loved working with the students and visiting them on their internships. I still have some classroom hours and would miss the teaching so it is the best of both worlds. I am told that I am very good but have learned to not pay too much attention to one's own "press" so I just try to do my best and not worry about the opinions of others.

There you have it, my life as a Vet Tech. I have loved almost every minute of it and have found that the students keep me on my toes.

How are you doing in terms of our meeting on Sunday? I am very excited and find that I can't sit idle for very long. How has my response to your 1st letter measured up to your expectations? I can easily imagine your greatest fear, but what about your greatest hope? I feel like I am living in a fairy tale. I have learned so much about you and have found so many connections, some of which are downright freaky!! The fact that everyone is so interested and supportive - I feel like Cinderella at the ball! I hope you are able to get some sleep tonight. Even Don is having trouble sleeping and this is the man who usually takes about 12 naps a day.

Love, Katie

PS - Tomorrow is the day I visit Camden Pet; I have never been there before so that is rather coincidental don't you think? See you Sunday!

Hi, Katie,

    Well, I am so impressed by your history as a veterinary technician that I am intimidated to say the least. And proud too, of course. It is fortunate to be able to make a living doing what you love.

    I have been consulting with a counselor for about a year and had an appointment today. She encouraged me to let myself go when we meet on Sunday. She knows that I am forever the stoic but I also know that I may not be able to keep it together when the time comes. Meanwhile I am concentrating on the business at hand.

    Tomorrow I will go plant shopping with a friend and Bill wants his last supper to be at Old Country Buffet. Then Saturday forenoon at about 11:00 I will see him off to the airport. After that I think I will go into the attic and dig for pictures. I don't know exactly what you would like to see but will try to bring a good variety. Then I will count the hours. I get so impatient. I hope we have a nice day for the park.

    I went to writing class tonight. The class is very small and we spent most of the time just gabbing. Intellectual gabbing mind you. I am trying to wind down. Less than three days.

Love, Jackie

Dear Jackie,

Well, I KNOW I won't be able to keep it together so no worries!! And yes, I too am planning on just letting it happen. It occurred to me that on Sunday our lives will be forever changed. I was "showing and telling" a dear person at work all about Sunday and she made a comment that didn't make sense at the time but now it makes perfect sense. She said, "Your future is going to begin on Sunday". A whole new world is going to open up and we do not know what it will hold however, we have the ability to make it whatever we want.

Our emails have even surprised me and I wrote half of them! Are you as amazed as I am at how much we have been willing to share in just 11 days? It just feels so honest. In a weird sort of way, it almost feels like I am talking to an older version of myself. And has it occurred to you that by reading our messages, how much Bill, like Don, has learned about the woman he has lived with all these years? Don is really enjoying it; I hope Bill is too. I love to hear Don's laugh from the other room when I know he is busy pouring over our messages. I have to quick run out and see who made him laugh - you or me! I think we are tied at this point!

Another thing I am looking forward to is that we have no rules. People who know you well are pretty astute at knowing what not to talk to you about (obviously!) while I have no idea what kind of questions would make your children or siblings gasp if they only knew! That will be part of the adventure. I am willing to talk about anything so don't hold back.

I am so amused that Bill wants to go to the Old Country Buffet. Veterinarians ALWAYS love a good buffet and I know of whence I speak! It sounds like you had a very good day in preparation for Sunday. A visit with your counselor followed by time spent with your writing group which must be VERY excited for you – WOW, which seems to be the word of the week!

I too, am glad to have plans for the next several days. Site visits and dinner with friends tomorrow night and as Saturday is Mom's birthday, I will be out shopping and taking her to dinner. I also plan to sit down and read our messages straight through from start to finish.

Good night my dear and rest well. The day is fast approaching although perhaps not fast enough? 50 years. . . .

Love, Katie

May 25-6, 2007

Hi, Katie,

What a nice letter. I hope you aren't getting all gooshey on me yet are you? With all due respect to your friend, I think our future started a couple of weeks ago but why quibble. It is the future that counts. My stomach is getting a little queasy as the hours pass. Or maybe it is just from OCB. Will we never learn?

I hope you are not disappointed but for my one big indiscretion I have lived a rather dull life. That is I have lived by the rules and my mother always said I was the easiest to raise. I bet she was disappointed. Truly, I did not rock the boat, I did not make waves. In other words not very colorful.

Did I mention that my friend Gretchen, who started me on this search, and some of her co-horts are going after the archdiocese for not initiating support groups for birth mothers. I think she is coming after me to help in this cause. They have support for women who have had abortions but have never acknowledged the price paid by birth mothers.

I came out to my friend Betty today, (that is 3 times this week) and she has a daughter who surrendered a child about 7 years ago. Her daughter knows where he is, sees him at least once a year and gets progress reports. And yet, Betty says, she does not get over the pain. Does it never get easier?

I was thinking today about that ride home from the hospital in 1957. I will share that when I see you. Are there any particular pictures you would like to see? I am afraid I will come loaded down if I don't have some guidelines here. Bill has always handled the picture taking chores and has been a little over zealous. Ever since it was discovered that he is good with a camera. I will try to be prudent.

By the way, how did your visit to Camden go? I have not seen the new facility but guess it would be an improvement. I always thought the other one was too small and claustrophobic.

I wish you a good day tomorrow with your mom. Bill will be gone by 11 so I will have time to prepare.

Love, Jackie

May 26, 2007

Dear Jackie,

Yes, as a matter of fact I am getting a little gooshey! And butterflies - I feel like there are about a million exiting their cocoons in my stomach. Last night I ate more in one sitting than I had in, oh . . . 12 days, and it sat in my stomach for hours like a chunk of concrete. I think that the closer I get to our meeting time, the more it becomes just about you and me and that is when I start to get very emotional. I must tell you about my day at the hospital for tests and this will make more sense but that story can wait. And when I refilled Winston's water dish this morning, I seemed to think that it belonged on the coffee table; somewhat akin to putting the mayo in the garage which cracked me up, by the way. I have no idea what happened to Monday's paper. . .

Pictures. I would like to see pictures of you and your immediate family; your children at various ages, your husband, and of course any pictures of you at any age. I would also like to see pictures of all of you together if you have any. And I must see a picture of your sister - the one who has always been in your face! Extended families and relatives can wait for another day. Let me know what you would like me to bring. I have so far gathered pictures of me at various ages and of course will bring the album that Dad put together. Many of these are baby pictures and as I have discovered from reading "the book", this may be difficult for you so you will need to let me know if you are ready to see them. I will happily let you take the album home to pore over and/or share with others. I am also collecting pictures of the people I have talked about in our emails; Mom, Dad, Mike and his wife, Todd and Lynn, many of which are group photos. I hope that helps you to cull the herd as they say in veterinary medicine.

Mike collected all the 8mm films that dad took of us as children which is not all that many, and transferred it to VHS format. I will try to track down my copy or borrow his so you can see me in motion as a child - hysterical if I may say so myself! The snow shoveling scene is priceless!

I had a very nice day of site visits yesterday. I started out at the Humane Society in Golden Valley and talked about our reconnection with my contact person there. She is adopted so we had quite a lively chat. My visit to Camden was interesting too. I had not seen the old clinic but am told that it was very close quarters so they are enjoying their new space. It is a lovely clinic but sorely in need of some art work on the walls which they are working on next.

Last night we had a very nice evening with my brother and his wife (Mike and Patty) and another couple who both have birthdays on Sunday. When I shared my news with them (more on that later), they pointed out to me that I will never forget their birthday in the coming years. May 27th will always be a special day from here on out.

I have not told you much about Mike and will take this opportunity to tell you a little bit about him. He will be 52 this August. I wouldn't say that we were particularly close when we were growing up but I don't know that I was really close to anyone until later in life. We had the usual sibling squabbles but oddly enough, he and my younger sister paired up even though there is a 7 year age difference between the two of them. Once Mike and I were in college and living away from home, we became much closer. We really seemed to connect in the past couple years and now see each other much more frequently.

Mike is very closed mouthed about pretty much anything having to do with feelings although he is very willing to share his opinions on just about everything and I say that with great affection. He has taken a little while to process this new information about me and is in a better place. One of his concerns I suspect is that he is afraid that he will lose me and family is VERY important to him. I am so happy to know that he has finally read all our emails and seemed to be in a very good place when I saw him last night. He is also very protective of Mom and was very worried about how she would handle this.

Mike married Patty when he was 42. They do not have any children and fill their time with bike rides, travel, and Gopher sporting events. Patty is a Gopher FREAK and I say that too, with affection. She is truly the light of his life and I am so happy that they eventually found each other. Mike is very frugal with the buck and was able to "retire" by the time he was 40 and believe me, he has taken a lot of crap for not working but has learned to handle that with humor. I had wondered what that must be like for Patty because she does work however, I have discovered that she actually has it made!! Mike does EVERYTHING! Housework, grocery shopping, cooking, (Patty is useless in the kitchen!) yard work, vehicle maintenance, windows, ironing, makes her lunch, takes her to work and oftentimes picks her up at the end of the day. Literally everything! When Patty comes home from work she does not have to do anything - how sweet is that! They are also able to travel whenever she has the time off from work. I think that Mike has a very rich life. He is very social by nature and they both have bonded with the coffee shop people who have welcomed us into their circle as well. I believe that Patty works because she must; she needs that outlet of being around other people and Mike obviously contributes to the household as previously listed.

The other couple we dined with last night is Doug and Joan from the coffee shop. I met them at Mike's 50th birthday party and Joan and I had an immediate connection as she too is adopted, just a few years younger than I am and we share a similar upbringing. I remember we talked at length about adoption that first time we met. For her birthday, I was wondering what to give her and decided to share our email correspondences with her (I have been copying and pasting our messages to one long document which runs to about 35 pages by the time I finish this message) and she was so touched. If she could have, I think she would have started reading them at the table last night. I suspect that when I see her this morning she will have read them all. I am so looking forward to her reactions and comments.

I just received an email from Lynn and must share her words of encouragement as it is very touching. *"Have fun Sunday, I will be thinking of you. Only I (and a few others) can tell you how wonderful it feels to be reborn!"* Once again, WOW!! Brief but oh so moving!

I suspect that by the time you read this, Bill has been dropped off at the airport and you are happy to have some time to yourself in preparation for our big day tomorrow. I will stay quite busy today with coffee group, visiting Dad, shopping for a gift for Mom and then gathering to celebrate her birthday. She has opened up so much in the past week that I expect tonight's gathering will the liveliest that we have ever had. I think we will all thank you one day for making all these wonderful things happen. I also think it will allow us (you and me) to build a genuine, lasting relationship that is of no threat to my family - beautiful!

I too am beginning to count down the hours and the emotions are so close to the surface as I write this so please excuse any typos. While I don't know what to expect (I have never done this before) I know that our meeting will be a wonderful, life changing event for both of us. I feel very safe with you and know in my head that I have nothing to fear. It is my heart and stomach that is creating the ruckus. My dearest hope is that you are in the same place. Sorry, but you must take the good with the gooshey on occasion! Which reminds me, I too was a very good child; no problems to raise, didn't make waves or create conflict within the family etc. If I had to do it all over again, I would have raised a little (make that a lot) more hell - I was way too easy on my parents!

I am reluctant to sign off as I so enjoy our connections through email so please keep them coming throughout the day and evening hours. I can't wait to touch you and share a good long cry that I suspect is way overdue for both of us! These past 12 days have been phenomenal however it will be so good to get to the point of meeting in person as I simply cannot maintain this high level of excitement and emotions for too much longer - it is exhausting. I cannot imagine how you, as the birth mother, must be feeling after waiting 50 years for tomorrow to arrive. I hope that the aftermath of our meeting is not too rough a road for you. I don't know what to expect but feel that it will be nothing but good!

See you tomorrow!

Love, Katie

Hi, Katie,

Bill does not need to be out of here until about 10:15. I just have to take him a couple miles over to his colleague's house and his wife will take the guys to the airport.

Yes I want to see pictures of your whole family. When I was an infant someone gave my mother one of those old Kodak box brownie cameras so she was very conscientious about keeping a record of our growth. A few years ago Bill put together some of the old 8mm films of our kids and put them on a DVD. If I can find it I will loan it to you. I also, as I may have mentioned, put together a "book" of my first 20 years, pictures and all and if you want to read that I will bring a copy also. I may have one you can have if you wish.

You can tell Mike not to worry that I will have any great impact on your family dynamics. I do not like to impose on anyone and would never try to inject myself into your lives as a family. I think you and I are on the same page there. (Now Bill could be something else but leave him to me.)

Right now I have my first load in the wash and will make a Target run sometime today. Tim is having us over on Monday and we will be celebrating my sister's birthday at the same time. The boys put on this humungous deck last summer so they have to make use of it.

One more idea I had is this: Someday I would like you and I to get together here and watch a film of DeLaSalle's production of COTTON PATCH GOSPEL. Have you ever seen this play? The music is by Harry Chapin and I needn't say more about that. It is a tear jerker for sure. Are we just going to become crying buddies do ya think? More later.

Love you, Jackie

Dear Jackie,

    I just returned from coffee and a long visit with my dad and Paula. It was a very nice morning and now I am off to run some errands.

    I managed to tear part of my bumper off the rear of the car while backing out of dad's driveway which I hate but as Winston was along, I didn't want to leave him parked on the street. Then I come home to a letter saying that Honda is looking for pre-owned vehicles at a sweet trade-in allowance and financing! Perhaps I can block their view of the right rear quarter panel! Oh well, I don't need a new car and have no fever at this time. Just butterflies. . .

Love, Katie

Hi, Katie,

    I spoke with Anne this afternoon. She has been very quiet on the subject and I have not shared e-mails as I wasn't sure of her stance. Anne is as private and close mouthed as I am at times. She did say something very interesting. She has always felt that there was a presence around her. Like maybe she was supposed to have a twin or something. I thought since she entered a uterus that had already been occupied; that someone had already imprinted for want of a better term. She said that now she knows the effect that you had on those that followed. Apparently there is someone at Holy Family who is proposing this theory. That is so weird. I am going to be thinking about that one for a long time. By the way, she visited Camden on Friday also. One of her cats has a bladder infection or some such.

Wouldn't it have been funny if the two of you had run into each other?

I am sorry to hear about your car. Now do I look for one with a bent fender? By the way, the sign says Community Activity Center. I just don't want to miss you.

I was so tired this afternoon I took a long nap. Rather late so I suppose I will be up half the night I am sure you enjoyed Joe's letter. He has a good sense of humor.

Not many hours left. I hope you sleep well after your big day today.

Love, Jackie

Dear Jackie,

I think there is a whole generation of adults born in the 40's, 50's and perhaps 60's who were all raised with the message that the possibility of reconnecting with birth parents is not a possibility. The adoptive parents were positively reassured that the information would remain secret and there was no chance of having the birth mother or father show up on the doorstep so to speak. Many of these children accepted that as a fact of life and so searching is not a part of their life plan.

I don't know anyone in my age group who has met their birth mother. On the other hand, Lynn has quite a few friends who have searched or been found and reunited. Several people have remarked on length of time (my age!) that has passed; I think they assume that it is done earlier in life or not at all. In any event, I think our timing couldn't be more perfect although I wish it didn't also represent how long you have wondered and waited and mourned. But tomorrow that will start to heal and come to an end eventually.

A friend has just stopped by so I best go be social. See you tomorrow and write again if you are up late as I expect I will be too!

Love, Katie

Hi, Katie,

My writing instructor has been mailing me. I don't think I told you this. She wanted to know when we are meeting as she wants to pray for us at that time; very nice of her. I know she will think this is a writing opportunity for me and will think that it is therapeutic as well. Will I need therapeutic?

Back to my pictures; it is so hard to choose. I just want to show you everything and tell you all about them but I realize that tomorrow isn't the only opportunity we will have.

Love, Jackie

Dear Jackie,

I say bring whatever you like; we may not get to any pictures although I doubt that. And as you say, this won't be our only opportunity to do so. I think that trying to cover 50 years in a day is an unrealistic expectation at best! I am being fairly frugal with my pictures because I think the special album will take some time and will quite likely provoke some sort of emotional response. I cry about how cute I was all the time! Okay, back to work for both of us! I am drinking coffee this evening so will be quite a heat source in bed tonight! Can't wait to touch you!

Katie

Hi, Katie,

I think I am finished with the pictures. Quite a conglomeration and more than you will care to see. Think I will turn in and try to sleep. It seems I wake at 6 anyway and can't go back to sleep. I can't wait to see the pix as a little one. See you tomorrow.

Love, Jackie

May 27, 2007

Good Morning my dear,

So, do you have any big plans for the day? This day is so big for me that I am actually going to reacquaint myself with the operations of an iron! My usual method is to throw the clothes in the dryer for a quick 10 minutes and blame any leftover wrinkles on my seatbelt.

What are you going to do between now and 1? I need to pick up the promised box of tissues and then will spend a lovely hour worshipping at the church of Mary - one of my oldest and dearest friends and one who has a fascination with adoption, both as a friend of an adoptee (me!) and as an adoptive parent. She is so excited that she can hardly string a sentence together these days. She makes me laugh and I miss her dearly as she lives in Chicago.

I received a message today that my email to Joe did not go through - there was one letter missing from the address. I have resent it and am so looking forward to seeing what he writes back. I am going to stop at Mom's on the way to Brooklyn Park to pick up that video I was telling you about and give her another reassuring hug that we will only get better! She is having up and down moments and hours but not days. And the ups are much more frequent than the downs.

I have a couple more emails to send this AM and will sign off now but will be checking frequently so please continue to respond. See you later TODAY!!!!!!!!!

Love, Katie

Hi, Katie,

Forget the iron. I did get to Mass this a.m. I woke at 5:30 and never did get back to sleep. So I talked myself out of the house and picked up coffee at Super America on the way home. I don't know why I dislike making coffee. And with Bill gone I can drop the work ethic. Now I am going to have breakfast and watch THIS WEEK. I only do it for the round table. That George Will is awesome. Also put some potatoes on to boil. They want my potato salad for tomorrow and I was wondering how I could get it all in. I am afraid I will fade by 2:00. There is little to be said for getting old. I try not to think too hard because I might start to cry too. So I am going to take to my chair for awhile now.

Love, Jackie

Dear Jackie,

I think yesterday was more difficult than today has been. I am glad that you are taking the time to put your feet up and relax. We have a big day ahead of us don't we? I find myself being very calm one moment and losing my head and temper the next. I even threatened Winston with euthanasia if he didn't "come in the house right now!" All in jest of course!!!!!!!!!!

I need to get to the place where it is just us! I am feeling overwhelmed with taking care of others (which is all self-inflicted and is my way) and answering so many questions from those who love me most. Fortunately they are all very understanding of how emotionally charged this day will be and so are not taking offense. I will see you very soon and am so looking forward to it!

Love, Katie

PS - I hope you were talking about being tired by 2:00 tomorrow and not today for I want more than an hour of your time!!

Katie,

Oh you will get all the time you/I need. It is just that if I don't answer some of your questions it could be that I have nodded off. It sounds like there are a lot of people rooting for you but it may be one of those times when you need to have a little quiet. I hope when this day is finished you can reassure your family that I am no threat. If you had told me to take a hike I'd have done so. Reluctantly, (heartbrokenly) but I'd have done it. Then we would really have missed THE DANCE wouldn't we?

Also, I am quite laid back so there is no need to be concerned about meeting. (Says she as her stomach goes into overdrive.) Better check them taters and eggs. Soon, very soon. Heehee!

Love, Jackie

Dear Jackie,

    I think my family already knows that to some degree but each has a process to go through in order to reach a place of peace and acceptance. Don reminded me to eat and the English muffin with peanut butter and jelly is just sitting in my stomach. I will sign off now so that the next time we communicate it will be in person!! See you very soon!

Love, Katie

Reunited!

You are undoubtedly anxious to hear about our first face-to-face meeting in over 50 years. I am afraid you may be disappointed as there were no violins playing or slow motion running through a field of flowers! However, you will enjoy reading of what did happen. In all actuality, our second meeting was much more profound for me than our first. I have discovered that this seems to be the case with other first meetings surrounding reunion. When I met some of my new sibs for the first time, it was great fun however, the second meeting was much more satisfying, insightful and indicated that we were really on our way to building lasting relationships.

Jackie

It was my first sight of Katie in 50 years. It was 1:00 on a Sunday afternoon in late May and the park was all but deserted. I pulled my car in next to hers and got out.

She was sitting at a picnic table. She was wearing an aqua blue dress and her blond head was bent forward, her face buried in her hands. My first thought was that she may be crying. As I walked across the park she got up and came toward me. Yes, definitely tear stains. We embraced and my first inclination was: "Don't cry. It will be all right." My own tears would have to wait.

We sat down opposite each other at the picnic table. I studied her face looking for some resemblance. It was beautiful. Her eyes were a blue that nearly matched her dress. Her hair was impossibly straight when one considers that curly and kinky come from all sides of the family. As we talked little images of long ago that I had forgotten kept coming through in expressions and gestures, always giving me a bit of a shock. "Oh yes, I had forgotten about that."

We talked the afternoon away. She filled me in on her diverse family. By late afternoon I learned about Don, Todd, Lynn, Mike, Patty, June, and most of the rest of the DeCosse's. I just couldn't remember where they all fit into this life that, until a few weeks ago, was unknown to me. My head was spinning but I still didn't know what she needed from me. Surely there was something after all of these years. But what?

When the sun became too much we got into my car and headed for Houlihan's. There we enjoyed a cocktail, probably an appetizer and brought out our stash of pictures. We enjoyed a meal and more hours of talking. I was afraid time was running out and I still didn't know what she needed from me. I kept asking but no answers were forthcoming. She was probably as puzzled as I was by that question. In retrospect, maybe it was I who was in need. Maybe I just wanted to be everything she wanted me to be. We had spent two weeks in intense e-mails and already knew quite a bit about each other yet in many ways still seemed like strangers to some extent. And maybe I was expecting too much too soon; afraid that this would slip away without something to hang onto.

Finally I drove her back to the park and she gave me one of her flower arrangements. I should have known then that I was "in like Flynn." (As we used to say.) Then she said she wanted to see me again. Soon. I had decided early on that I would let her orchestrate this reunion as I wouldn't interfere with or interrupt her life in any way. I just wanted to be there for whatever she needed. And I STILL didn't know what THAT was.

One might expect that this was the climax of the reunion. And for some adoptees and mothers, it is. For us it was only the beginning. Not only did we want to know more about each other, we wanted to know about those years that we had been separated.

I can still see that picture in my mind: The park with the white pagoda, green picnic table, flower gardens, sweeping lawn, and her sitting there; the short blond hair, the blue eyes and that beautiful smile.

Katie

Our first meeting has come and gone. The weather couldn't have been more perfect; the sun was out, the temperature was perfect with little humidity and we had the privacy that I sought. I arrived first and about 20 minutes early so was able to choose the spot where we would sit and visit for the first time in 50 years.

After signing off for the last time, I did indeed stop at Mom's. It was important for me to have that send off of love and support; I was taking the next step in a journey that could go anywhere, or nowhere. Once I was on my way to our designated meeting spot, all the stress, excitement, and apprehension of the previous 12 days simply melted away. At last, there was no one who needed "taking care of" except me.

I proceeded on my way to the park. It was empty! No cars, no people, just me in the midst of greenery and sunshine. I chose one of several picnic tables available and settled in to wait.

How does one even begin to describe an encounter such as this? I was about to meet, for the first time, the woman who gave me life; the one who had made a decision 50 years earlier that impacted both of our lives and many others as well. The person I was about to meet is the one who equipped me with the skills to carry out my part of our shared assignment. At one time this person must have been so familiar to me; after all we had shared nine months together before I slipped out to begin a journey that would not include Jackie. It took 50 years for our paths to cross again and now our first face-to-face meeting was about to take place.

What WAS I expecting that day? My recurring dream had Jackie dressed in a royal blue evening gown, however I was not expecting *that*. Although I had seen pictures of Jackie, I was still expecting a miraculous resemblance. I knew I was about to meet the person with whom I had shared so much of myself in such a short amount of time. Through these exchanges I had discovered someone very much like me and I just knew we would have a delightful day together.

Jackie told me what kind of car she drove so I knew immediately when she had arrived. I have come to discover that it takes her forever to gather her things and get out of the car and this day was no different. I recall sitting with my hands on my face watching her approach. I knew beyond a doubt that we were genetically connected – our emails had demonstrated that. Now was my chance to see *and* hear someone, for the first time ever, with whom I shared DNA. As she moved closer, I found myself already looking for physical resemblances.

I knew her with my heart but not as a living breathing person, who moves and speaks and laughs. Discovering this Jackie began that day as we shared a long overdue embrace. When I looked closely into her face, there were no tears. Oddly enough, I did not break down in tears, but there were a few. To this day I wish I could recall exactly, her first words to me. The closest I can remember is, "So, is this what you were expecting?"

Our afternoon and evening together was an almost surreal experience. The rest of the world simply disappeared and it was just the two of us, as it had once been so many years ago. I needed to connect in my mind that the person I had spent days getting to know via email was in fact, the woman sitting across from me. She is my mother. And yet, I have a mother. I know what she looks like. Jackie was another mother to me. Shouldn't there be an innate recognition of this?

Since our first meeting, I have discovered that all first meetings are awkward to some degree. If it were up to me, we would skip the first and go directly to the second. Our next visit proved to be the one where I *knew* we were connected; that she was indeed the one who gave birth to me and our bond was still intact. The following is part of a message that I sent Jackie several days after our second meeting.

I can hardly begin to tell you how much I enjoyed seeing you on Wednesday evening. We laughed - A LOT!! It felt more comfortable than Sunday, although not to take anything away from Sunday which was special in its own right by nature of being our first meeting. On Wednesday, I began to see myself in you for the first time and that was very magical. I saw my interest in and concern for others reflected back at me; I saw my tough side - the part of me that doesn't need any help, I can take care of myself; and I saw the fun side, of me in you! She's in there and I want to get to know her better too! I wasn't expecting this strong connection so soon in our relationship and I am enjoying every second of it.

And that is how our journey began. This has indeed been the experience of a lifetime. We continue to see each other frequently and have reached a place where we are secure in the relationship we have built. Yes, "it could have been so much worse", but I prefer to say that "It could not have been better!"

Afterword

Almost 2 years have elapsed since we embarked on this journey of reunion. Hopefully many of your questions will be answered in the following pages.

"Shortly after the meeting, Katie left her teaching position to work toward her Master's degree. It gave us plenty of time to spend together. That was one of the gifts this reunion produced. We were able to spend a lot of time together, building our own history and traditions. We wasted no time. Over the next several months, we lunched, we talked, and we explored new territories together. We have many of the same interests. We both like to read, crochet, visit on my patio and take walks. And we both like Toby Keith. She is the only one of my children that shares my interest in country music."

While everything seemed like a fairy tale on the outside, underneath it all, there were people trying to push us along and those who were still reluctant to participate. We seemed to be caught in the middle and had the task of keeping things under control while trying to move ahead at our own pace.

This experience has challenged us in many ways: What to do about holidays? What are the ground rules in this new relationship? How is conflict resolved? What do we call each other? When and how do we introduce each other to our families? Some of these issues have been completely resolved while others remain works in progress. One thing we have discovered is that with an open mind and heart, we can always find our way.

"Katie had five new siblings to meet; some willing and anxious, others more reluctant. We each have a spouse, each one more excited than the other about our progress, on the sidelines and cheering. Then there were my siblings, aunts and uncles chomping at the bit to meet this new niece. The one they had known about for years. The one hidden in the shadows of our history..."

Tom, Katie and Tim

"I have built long-lasting relationships with two of my "new" brothers. They have added so much fun, interest and laughter to this reunion journey. Siblings are indeed a bonus!"

Extended family has now been included in our reunion experience. Most introductions were made in large groups. Since first meetings seem to be awkward, this was a way to get a whole bunch of them over with at once! And then we had all those fun second meetings to look forward to.

Jackie, Sharon, Katie, Kathy and Richard

"Jackie had warned me of her siblings' interest in meeting me but I was not prepared for the immediate and warm inclusion into their world. Kathy's brunch will always be one of my fondest memories of this reunion journey."

In September we rented a cabin in northern Minnesota and were able to spend an entire week together, something that we had never had a chance to do. All our fears were for naught as it ended up being one of the most magical weeks of our reunion.

"I would have to say that my favorite memory of that first year is what I refer to as "the cabin at the

lake." That September we spent a week at a cabin on a little lake near Pine River. It was so quiet and peaceful. We brought Winston along in case we needed a tension defuser. We took several long walks on The Paul Bunyan Trail. We went for massages, shopped for books and candles, and journaled to each other during the quiet times. We ate chocolate and watched movies. In the morning we would bundle up to drink coffee on the porch and quietly watch the sun come up. In the evening Katie might make a bonfire and we bundled up to sit outside and just talk. We discovered that neither one of us is immune to clutter. We didn't know if we could last the whole week together and then found it was not enough time."

"When asked to describe what this week was like for me, I discovered that it was like spending time with an older version of me. It was an unbelievable week."

I am sure you are wondering if Jackie and Mom have met and the answer is "Yes!" About four months into our reunion (9/07), they both decided that they were able to take this step.

"And then there was her mom. How do I explain what I felt for this woman? She was my counterpart. I would like to think she took my place in Katie's life but that doesn't seem right and wouldn't be fair to her. She did not do this for me, nurture and care for Katie. She is Katie's mom and Katie is her daughter. Does she resent my showing up in her life? Does she view me as an interloper? I tried to imagine how I would feel if I thought someone came to. . . what? . . . Reclaim my daughter? . . . Her daughter? I would not blame her if she felt that way. I needed to prove that I was no threat. And time would take care of that."

"I hosted a brunch in my home as that made me most comfortable; neutral territory so to speak. This worked well for all of us. As is typical of a first meeting, it was slightly awkward but not nearly as uncomfortable as I was afraid it might be. Both were extremely gracious and friendly towards each other. Coincidentally, Jackie was leaving soon for her first trip to Italy and Mom has been many times so we spent quite a bit of time on that topic."

Jackie, Katie and Mom

Holidays took care of themselves as we had decided that they shouldn't change. We have many of our own traditions and will continue with those. It was fun to discover that Christmas Eve was available to both of us so that has become our special time of celebration.

"We were able to navigate the holidays without changing anything but for Christmas Eve. In recent years, Katie and Don, Tom and Tim, and Bill and I *spent the evening in our own homes. That first year we decided to spend Christmas Eve together for a home cooked meal and an evening of fun and sharing. We had started a new tradition."*

Other special days have come and gone. We have celebrated birthdays, Valentine's Day, and are approaching our second Mother's Day together. We invented new holidays too. May 14th is now Letter Day and Meeting Day will always be May 27th.

"Our first Mother's Day celebration was derailed when Jackie suffered a medical emergency the weekend prior to this important holiday, especially in the first year of reunion. Rather than do anything extravagant, we simply spent a lovely midday basking in the spring time sun of early May. We laughed and talked. I was just so happy to have a little bit of time to make sure she was going to be okay. To simply see, feel and touch her was all that I needed. I will always recall the joy of that simple little celebration."

This entire reunion experience has been far beyond anything we could have possibly imagined, predicted or hoped for. The inclusion of others in our journey has been a powerful gift to give as well as receive. It has been the chance of a lifetime and we have enjoyed just about every minute of it. In the coming years, we expect the newness will wear off but the relationships will deepen and continue to enrich all our lives.

Transitions

It has been two years now since I sent the letter. It has been said that these reunions are like a rebirth and that the ongoing relationship goes through many of the phases that a mother and child experience under natural circumstances. During this time our relationship has evolved from being all consuming to something more normal. It has been like stepping into a time warp. In two years time we have developed a relationship with all of the characteristics of same that most people do in eighteen. In other words, we have been on fast forward.

We have gone through all of the phases of a mother/daughter bonding process. Two years ago it felt just like getting to know a newborn. We were wrapped up in finding out about each other. Exploring and examining physical and personality similarities. We both possessed an innate curiosity that hungered to be satisfied. The bonding came naturally but the connections had to be put in place.

That first year was filled with making history; establishing traditions, and acquainting ourselves with members of our extended families. We also took much time away from others to get to know each other. We were lucky in that we had so much support from friends and family. They never doubted that we would be back and that we needed this time. They too, were fascinated with this process and for the most part were experiencing it along with us. It was as new to them as to us.

Then suddenly and without warning, a transition seemed to be taking place. The newness seemed to have disappeared and what was to take its place? Frightening! Where do we go from here? We had talked together, laughed together, lunched and vacationed together. Everything was new, until now. Would it all end? Were we destined to separate again? That was scary.

As it turned out, we had built our relationship on a firm foundation. Neither one of us wanted to let go of what we had. We just needed to loosen the grip on the bond that had formed between us. We were more confident that this time it would hold.

The next several months were a period of settling in. Gradually we were taking back our old life; spending more time with friends and working on this book. We had made a pact early on to be open with each other. We would share anything and everything with which we felt comfortable. While the first months seemed to find us in perfect sync, we were now able and even found it necessary to put voice to our discontent. Much of this stemmed from outside forces but we didn't want anything to stand between us in the way of conflict. Maybe we were expecting too much. We were now confident that small matters would not tear us asunder even if they were painful.

Now we are in what I refer to as our period of adolescence. I am no longer the center of her world. Her horizons are expanding. She is making new friends and meeting new, younger and more exciting family members. I sometimes feel myself drifting away into an outer circle; the one occupied by my generation.

We are also picking up the threads of our former lives. The trust we have built allows us to loosen our grip on the bond that does and always will connect us. We now have the time to renew old friendships, pursue new career paths, and develop new interests. I believe this is as it should be. As a parent, I have learned that there is a time to let go, the emptying of the nest. I always had trouble with that but she is not far away.

She may weave in and out of my life as the others do. We knew early on that we could not recapture those fifty years of separation but we have endeavored in the last two years, to embrace this new relationship as fully as possible. We worked hard to build a strong relationship. I think we have done well.

Rebirth

Almost two years have passed since I received Jackie's letter. It is said that "timing is everything"; our reunion experience has convinced me of the truth in those three little words. I never really thought that I would ever meet my birth mother and so never imagined that it could be such a life-changing event.

Only an adoptee can really understand the following statement: One of the things we miss most is what everyone else takes for granted: knowing people through a biological connection. Being surrounded by people with genetic similarities in how they look, act and think is not part of our history. Occasionally this difference was apparent but it was not a daily concern of mine. In wasn't until our reunion that I realized what I had really been missing all those years.

Reuniting with Jackie and meeting all these new relatives has taught me so much about myself. Validation is a word that frequently comes to mind when I reflect on why this information has made such a difference in my life. Some traits can be explained away as coincidence while others can only be explained through genetics. What other reason could there be for our nearly identical laugh or the similarities in our writing styles? I have always been a bit of a loner – I like my solitude; I have discovered that there are a lot of loners on this new family tree. This provides more pieces to the puzzle that has made me the person I am today. It explains many of the choices I have made in my life in the ensuing years since my placement in 1957. Reunion has surrounded me with people who innately understand me; they "get" me so to speak. That is something I never expected to find.

The timing for this validation and accompanying insights could not have been more perfect. I was already at an age of empowerment and eager to discover all I could about myself. Reunion provided the vehicle for me to become the person I was always meant to be; it has filled in many of the blanks and has given me a new confidence in myself.

Through reuniting with Jackie, I have also gained a new sense of belonging. I already have a family I belong to; now I understand where I belong genetically as well. History cannot be duplicated or rewritten; I will always be a DeCosse and that is as it should be. Reunion has provided me with the opportunity to build another "history" with whatever time is left and with anyone willing to take the risk. It has also given me the self-confidence to renew and repair other relationships in my life and that has been a wonderful and unexpected benefit of our journey.

If you are an adoptee, I encourage you to consider pursuing a reunion. Comparatively speaking, there are not that many of us so it is a very select group that will even have the opportunity for an experience such as ours. I have a difficult time imagining what my life journey would look like without this reconnection along the way. And that could very easily have happened, if it had been left up to me.

Fortunately, Jackie took the bold step of reaching out to me so birth mothers might also consider searching. You are part of an elite and dwindling group of people:

those women who placed a child in the era of closed adoptions. It is a far different world these days.

Speaking on behalf of the children you surrendered, we feel little, if any, animosity toward you. Many of us are at a place in our lives where we have more time to pursue other interests; children are grown and gone and retirement approaches. There is a mellowing with age that may be more conducive to sustaining a reunion; one that can more easily be built on trust and respect. It is easier to ask the questions that we wouldn't have dreamt of asking in our 20's or 30's.

With the knowledge and insights that occur through reunion, there is an enormous potential for healing, growth and joy, for both the parent and child. Letting go of shame, finding the answers to long-held questions, and discovering those similarities that can only be explained through genetics, is the ultimate reward for the risk of reunion.

Many months ago Lynn so aptly wrote, *"Only I (and a few others) can tell you how wonderful it feels to be re-born!"* I have come to agree wholeheartedly with her statement; it is wonderful! Being re-born at 50 with the ability to verbalize all the thoughts, feelings and emotions is a profound journey of the heart, mind and soul; if at all possible, an experience not to be missed.

Acknowledgments

A journey such as ours could not have taken place without the support and encouragement of many people. From the moment that Jackie's search began in earnest through the completion of this book, many people have helped us along the way.

First and foremost, we thank those members of our families – immediate and extended - who have been so patient, understanding and willing to participate in this magical journey of reunion. To be so warmly welcomed into each other's lives has been an unexpected bonus. Without this love and support, our reunion would have been much more difficult.

Friends have always been an important part of each of our lives. Their patience and understanding as we each disappeared for months at a time, in order to explore this new relationship, is something we appreciate beyond words. The title of this book actually came from a special group of friends and to them we say, "Thank You!" You know who you are!

Many people read the early editions of this book and we would not have gone forward with this project without their interest, encouragement and feedback. At one point, this book was much longer so some of these readers have done some hard time and for that we are most appreciative. One day the rest of the story will be told so please know your efforts were not in vain.

We extend a special "Thank You" to Cy DeCosse for providing the photos for the cover and putting it all together. It ended up being much more difficult than one might expect but well worth the effort!

Without the help of searchers, this journey would never have taken place. We thank them for their assistance, perseverance and willingness to help us find each other.

Lastly, we thank our spouses who were most impacted by this event. They saw less of us, ate more take-out, and stood back so that we could let our hearts lead the way in this journey of search, discovery, and recovery.

> We would like to hear from you! If you have any comments, questions, concerns or stories to tell, please feel free to contact us. Your letters should be addressed to:
> Wow! Publishing Group,
> 2359 Cleveland Street NE,
> Minneapolis, MN 55418
>
> Our website, www.wowpublishinggroup.com will be up and running by May 1, 2009. We look forward to your email messages.
>
> Thank you for your interest!
>
> *Jackie* and **Katie**

Made in the USA